D1106122

PREFERRED STOCK INVESTING
Fourth Edition

By
Doug K. Le Du

Doug K. Le Du publishes two preferred stock research newsletters – the *CDx3 Newsletter* and *CDx3 Research Notes*.

The purchase of *Preferred Stock Investing* includes a subscription to the *CDx3 Newsletter*. The *CDx3 Newsletter* is emailed to readers each month and is free to you. The *CDx3 Newsletter* provides preferred stock investing news, tips, questions and answers from the author and much more.

To activate your free subscription to the *CDx3 Newsletter* send an email message to:

CDx3Newsletter@PreferredStockInvesting.com

CDx3 Research Notes is available to subscribers to the CDx3 Notification Service – a research and email notification service for preferred stock investors (see www.PreferredStockInvesting.com).

The preferred stock research data for this book was gathered between 2006 and May 2011. Chapter 15 presents the investment results, using the CDx3 Income Engine method explained throughout this book, for all qualifying preferred stocks issued between January 2001 and December 2010.

As a reader of *Preferred Stock Investing* you are entitled to free periodic updates to the preferred stock lists provided in chapter 15. To receive the most recent update, follow the instructions at the beginning of chapter 15.

Copyright © 2011 Doug K. Le Du

ISBN-13 978-1-60145-163-7
ISBN-10 1-60145-163-6

All rights reserved. No part of this publication may be reproduced, stored in a retrieval system, or transmitted in any form or by any means, electronic, mechanical, recording or otherwise, without the prior written permission of the author.

Printed in the United States of America

CD Times Three trademark of Doug K. Le Du
CDx3 trademark of Doug K. Le Du
CDx3 Income Engine trademark of Doug K. Le Du
CDx3 Investor trademark of Doug K. Le Du
CDx3 Key Rate Chart trademark of Doug K. Le Du
CDx3 Portfolio trademark of Doug K. Le Du
CDx3 Preferred Stock trademark of Doug K. Le Du
CDx3 Perfect Market Index trademark of Doug K. Le Du
CDx3 Bargain Table trademark of Doug K. Le Du
Preferred Stock List trademark of Doug K. Le Du

The company logos used throughout this book are trademarks of the indicated companies.

Disclaimer: The content of this book is educational rather than advisory. This book explains a method to assist you in making investment decisions. Neither this book, nor Doug K. Le Du nor the PreferredStockInvesting.com website provides personal investment advice. There can always be exceptions to the trends and generalizations presented here. The reader, and not Doug K. Le Du, is responsible for considering the educational information presented here and making their own investment decisions in light of their personal financial resources, goals and risk tolerance.

Cover: Brian Bell, Gary Rosing (photo)
Published in the United States by Booklocker.com, Inc.
4.01.

ACKNOWLEDGEMENTS

First and foremost, I thank my wife Jan who not only listened with unlimited patience for many months to my thoughts on every aspect of this project, but was always ready to apply the diligence of a corporate Controller to my work.

I thank Dr. E. J. Le Du, my father, who first interested me in preferred stock investing and, with decades of experience investing in them, is a preferred stock investor extraordinaire.

Mr. J. Steven Carrillo is one of those unique individuals who has a thirst and passion for all things related to investing. After reading a research paper I had written on preferred stock investing, several people urged me to write this book – none more ardently than Steve. I remain in his debt on many fronts.

Mr. Brian Bell added his creative talents and unique eye for design to the book cover. I remain very grateful for his work.

I would like to thank Dr. Catherine Finger. While any remaining calculation errors are mine, Dr. Finger shed the harsh light of a university accounting professor on the key calculations that are used throughout this book.

I also wish to thank Mr. Karel Podolsky, former corporate finance instructor at Portland State University, whose expertise with financial calculations in general, and Microsoft Excel worksheet functions in particular, was a huge help in many ways.

And a big thank you goes to my readers and subscribers who, since 2003 when I wrote my first research paper regarding preferred stock investing, have provided many thoughts, comments, questions, insights and encouragement. I am thankful to receive your supportive email messages every day and please know that I read them all. I am hopeful that you find my continued commitment to preferred stock research interesting and helpful.

FORWARD

The only problem with bank Certificates of Deposit (CDs), as far as I can see, is that you never seem to make any real money from them. One day I "ran the numbers." By the time you subtract income taxes and inflation, you've wiped out much (if not all) of your CD's interest income. Once I realized this fact, CDs became as comfortable as an ice cream headache.

Take this common example: say you buy a 12-month bank CD for $1,000 that pays 2% annual interest. You're going to make $20 in interest income from this CD. But that $20 is subject to income tax. Let's say the income tax rate is a combined (federal plus state) 40%; so, subtract $8 off of your $20 for income taxes. Now you're down to $12. After twelve months, inflation eats away another 2% of your $1,000. So you lose another $20 to inflation. Subtracting this $20 out of your remaining $12, and guess what – you've just lost $8 on that 2% CD.

And yet bank CDs are sold as low risk money makers every day.

With all of the investments that the U.S. economy offers us, doesn't it seem like there would be a way to make a respectable return at acceptable risk?

My background in economics, statistics and as a Managing Director at one of the world's largest management consulting firms provided me with the tools to answer that question. It took some doing to be sure – years actually.

But look at the results:

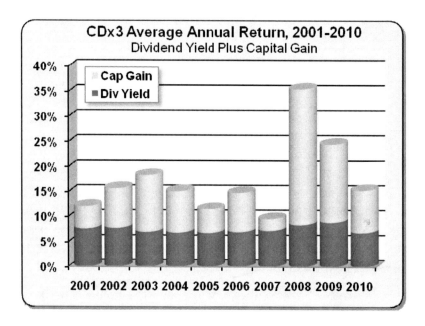

By selecting, buying and selling the highest quality preferred stocks as described throughout this book you can collect fixed quarterly dividend income plus pile on a nice capital gain (if you so choose) downstream. The result is a return that is several times what bank CDs can earn.

That's why I call my preferred stock investing method the "CD Times Three Income Engine" or "CDx3" for short.

The method for selecting the highest quality preferred stocks that I describe in chapter 7 successfully filtered out the preferred stocks from every failed bank during the Global Credit Crisis that started in June 2007.

By investing in the manner described in this book, the CDx3 Income Engine promotes low risk investors out of the low-to-no return garbage heap into the comfortable sunshine of respectable returns at acceptable risk.

And, in this book, I'm going to teach you how to do it.

TABLE OF CONTENTS

Doug K. Le Du

INTRODUCTION

There's no shortage of investment books out there; so, first, I want to thank you for buying this one. You'll be very glad you did.

The investing method described throughout this book is called the "CD Times Three" Income Engine or "CDx3" Income Engine for short.

The CDx3 Income Engine: Use the highest quality preferred stocks to earn above average dividend income while simultaneously creating multiple downstream capital gain opportunities.

The CDx3 Income Engine has consistently delivered returns that are well beyond those that are possible with bank CDs, hence the name CDx3.

I am about to teach you how to screen, buy and sell the highest quality preferred stocks regardless of what interest rates or inflation are doing.

The ten selection criteria presented in chapter 7 filter out about 90 percent of the preferred stocks trading on today's stock market. In fact, these ten criteria successfully filtered out the preferred stocks from all of the failed banks during the Global Credit Crisis that began during the summer of 2007 – IndyMac, New Century, Fannie Mae, Freddie Mac, Lehman Brothers, Bear Stearns, Washington Mutual, CIT Group – all of them.

The ten CDx3 Selection Criteria that you will learn about in chapter 7 were specifically designed to meet the three objectives of the CDx3 Income Engine: (1) maximize revenue while (2) minimizing risk and (3) minimizing work.

Stock investing books have a lot of similarities – most tell you that if you buy certain stocks under certain conditions then sell them later under certain conditions you will make lots of money.

This investment book, *Preferred Stock Investing,* departs from all others in two ways:

1) This investing book shows you how to make a respectable rate of return (several times what bank CDs can give you) using "investment grade" preferred stocks, not common stocks, bonds or mutual funds; and

2) This investing book uses examples to educate you on how the CDx3 approach works but unlike other investment books, I will subject every CDx3 Preferred Stock issued since January 2001 to the CDx3 Income Engine and show you, in detail, the results. Then you can decide for yourself how well it works. Some authors essentially ask you, the reader, to take their word that their approach really works. Others present a few very carefully selected examples to

support their case. I'm not going to ask you to take my word for it; I'm not going to cherry pick a few choice examples that happen to fit. You'll see the results in chapter 15.

The CDx3 Income Engine approach does not even require much of your time. No more time than you would spend looking at your monthly bank statement.

You will not have to become a "day trader" continually hunched over your computer studying arcane charts. Besides, did you know that over 70% of day traders lose money? But for every loser, there's a winner and we're going to be on the right side of that deal – making the money.

And by the time you've finished reading this book you'll know when (right down to the day and in advance) to do your trades and at what price. Skeptical? Keep reading.

The investment approach described throughout this book – the CDx3 Income Engine – is for investors looking to earn several times the return on money that they would otherwise be investing in CDs, bonds or Treasury Notes – other low risk investment instruments; although, you don't want to say that CDs are "low risk" to people who had their life savings in CDs at many savings and loans in the 1980's – what a meltdown.

The CDx3 Income Engine is *NOT* for investors who need a current income portfolio that generates something north of twenty-five percent in order to stay afloat. That type of return is very difficult to attain and involves a much higher degree of risk than CDx3 Investors are comfortable with.

Having said that, I would encourage any investor or investment group to dedicate at least a portion of their holdings to a CDx3

Portfolio. The CDx3 Income Engine approach relies on relatively safe, fixed-income preferred stocks that meet very specific selection criteria and, when bought and sold using the approach I'm about to describe to you, generate a substantially better return than CDs or bonds. But it's never going to be twenty or thirty percent and it would be irresponsible for me to say, or for you to believe, otherwise.

The Dow Jones Industrial Average (DJIA) opened on January 2, 2001 at 10,646 and, after reaching a high of 14,154 in October 2007, closed on December 31, 2010, ten years later, at 11,578 (source: *MarketWatch.com*). By investing in the common stock market, as reflected by the DJIA, you would have made about $900 (less than one percent per year) on the original $10,646 that you invested ten years earlier.

CDx3 Preferred Stocks issued between January 2001 and December 2010, on the other hand, generated annual returns in the range of 10% to 35%[1] year in and year out (see page 224 for annual values).

So when I say that the CDx3 Income Engine is an investment approach based on the highest quality preferred stocks ("CDx3 Preferred Stocks") I hope that you are starting to get an idea of what I'm talking about.

Throughout This Book

There are a variety of terminology and other conventions that I use throughout this book.

Historical Market Prices

Historical market price data is only available for securities that are currently trading. The original data for this book was gathered in 2006

---

[1] The 35% value was a non-typical result of the Global Credit Crisis.

and periodically updated since then through March 2011. Since CDx3 Preferred Stocks have a five year life span[2], the oldest available historical market price for them begins in January 2001.

Effective Annual Return Calculations

In order to calculate the effective annual return of an investment, one needs to know, among a few other things, the purchase price and the sell price of that investment.

These prices will vary depending on market conditions so, for the purposes of this book, I use the following conventions when calculating the effective annual return:

1) The purchase price of CDx3 Preferred Stocks purchased during a "seller's market" (described later) is set to $25.00 per share (even though you will purchase them for less than this as you will soon see);

2) The purchase price of CDx3 Preferred Stocks purchased during a "buyer's market" (also described later) is set to the closing market price on the first trading day following the second dividend quarter (the reasons why will become clear once your read about purchasing preferred stocks during buyer's market conditions in chapter 10); and

3) The sell price is set to the actual closing market price on the day that you would have sold your CDx3 Preferred Stock if you had been following the CDx3 Income Engine method as described throughout this book. Note that the most recently issued CDx3 Preferred Stocks at the time this edition is being written have yet to be sold.

---

[2] IPO date to call date.

Interest Or Dividends

Most of the cash that you receive from preferred stocks is classified for tax purposes as either dividend income or interest income. For simplicity, throughout this book I refer to the cash you receive each quarter from your CDx3 Preferred Stock investments as "dividend" income.

Your broker will perform a reconciliation at the end of each year and provide you with the proper IRS 1099 form that classifies your income. You can also refer to the prospectus of your preferred stock for this classification or contact the issuing company. Just remember, the authority to classify your investment income lies solely with the U.S. Internal Revenue Service, not your broker and not the issuing company.

Next Week's Grocery Money

Like any investment, reaping a return assumes that the entity you are investing in stays in business. While there has never been a case where the issuing company of a CDx3 Preferred Stock has gone out of business, this is not to say that it cannot happen or that it never will happen.

Market prices of preferred stocks fluctuate over time (frequently with changes in interest rates). Money that you invest in the stock market should be long-term money that you can use to take advantage of these swings. Investing is no place for next week's grocery money.

The CDx3 Income Engine relies on buying at the right time, then selling at the right time and knowing how to recognize the right conditions when they are upon you. The right selling conditions may be several quarters downstream so there may be times when some patience is in order. Remember though that you'll be earning above average dividend income in the meantime.

Recommendations And Advice

Never invest your money based on advice from someone who is not familiar with your investment goals, resources and risk tolerance.

CDx3 Preferred Stocks are regular preferred stocks that meet the ten CDx3 Selection Criteria presented in chapter 7. They are not to be taken as recommendations to buy or not to buy. How well a specific CDx3 Preferred Stock meets your individual investment needs is a decision that only you can make. My purpose here is to help you make more informed decisions regarding your preferred stock investments.

Website References

Website references presented throughout this book were current at the time this edition of *Preferred Stock Investing* was written in early 2011. But please note that the public and private organizations that own these websites may change their web address or content at any time.

If you use the website references presented herein and get that annoying "website not found" message, the site has probably moved to another address. Using your favorite search engine to locate the new address should get you back under way.

Summary Of The CDx3 Income Engine

Here is the CDx3 Income Engine in a nutshell:

> **The CDx3 Income Engine:** Use the highest quality preferred stocks to earn above average dividend income while simultaneously creating multiple downstream capital gain opportunities.

The CDx3 Income Engine uses a combination of dividend income and capital gain income to produce great returns. Annual dividend rates paid by CDx3 Preferred Stocks are between 6.5% and 9%. Selling downstream for a capital gain pushes your effective annual return the rest of way – generally well over 10% (chapter 15 presents the investing results for every CDx3 Preferred Stock issued since January 2001).

If you want to purchase CDx3 Preferred Stocks for their very respectable 6.5% to 9% annual dividend income and leave it at that, great. But what if you could earn much more than that without additional risk or effort? That's where the CDx3 Income Engine comes in.

CDx3 Investors buy their CDx3 Preferred Stocks at a point in time when research shows the market price tends to be relatively low, less than $25.00 per share, and hold their CDx3 Preferred Stocks until:

1) You can sell for the Target Sell Price (chapter 13); or

2) The issue is "called" (bought back from you) by the issuing company (if so, they are required to pay you $25.00 per share regardless of your original purchase price).

Either way, CDx3 Investors buy for less than $25 per share and sell for at least $25 per share so you are positioned to realize a capital gain in addition to the above average dividend income in the meantime.

So the question becomes how to buy for less than $25 per share regardless of market conditions and how do you know when to look for the Target Sell Price or the arrival of the call date (much more on this in chapters 13 and 14). And that's what this book is going to teach you how to do and show you the results.

Here is a table that summarizes what you are going to learn about the CDx3 Income Engine throughout this book. While the information on this table may be foreign to you now, by the time you finish this book you will have a keen understanding of all of its entries.

The CDx3 Income Engine Summary Table

	CDx3 MARKETPLACE DIRECTION	
	Buyer's Market	**Seller's Market**
HOW TO TELL (Part I)	• Dividend rates increasing • Market prices < $25 per share • CDx3 Perfect Market Index >100	• Dividend rates decreasing • Market prices > $25 per share • CDx3 Perfect Market Index <100
SELECTING (Part II)	• CDx3 Selection Criteria • SEC EDGAR system • Watchlist (one for each quarter) • CDx3 Preferred Stock catalog	• CDx3 Selection Criteria • SEC EDGAR system • Watchlist (one for each quarter) • CDx3 Preferred Stock catalog

BUYING
(Part III)
	• New issues > Over-The-Counter
	• CDx3 Bargain Table
	  - < $25 per share
	  - Early in dividend quarter
	  - Old issues > 2nd dividend qtr
	• Big Bank TRUPS
	• CDx3's Beyond Call Date
		• New issues > Over-The-Counter
		• CDx3 Bargain Table
		  - < $25 per share
		  - Early in dividend quarter
		
		• Big Bank TRUPS
		• CDx3's Beyond Call Date

SELLING (Part IV)	• Enjoy dividend checks; do not sell during a buyer's market • Check for "upgrades"	• Market price > Target Sell Price; or • Called by issuing company for $25 • Last day of dividend quarter • Check for "upgrades"

We will be revisiting this table as I explain each aspect of the CDx3 Income Engine to you.

Specifically, this book is organized into five parts that will describe how you, as a preferred stock investor, can put the CDx3 Income Engine to work for you.

Part I: The Preferred Stock Market

Part I of this book provides you with an explanation of the preferred stock market including what a preferred stock is, the three types of preferred stocks, how they differ from other fixed-income investments and how a new preferred stock is created and comes to market.

But the most important topic of Part I will be found in chapter 3 – The Three Rules of Market Price Predictability. These are the three rules that push the market price of CDx3 Preferred Stocks in the short-term of one dividend quarter, the longer-term over the life span of the security and what I call the end-term once the preferred stock can be retired by the issuing company.

The Three Rules of Market Price Predictability are what make the CDx3 Income Engine run and I'll show you several examples of these three rules in action throughout this book.

Part II: Selecting The Highest Quality Preferred Stocks

To qualify as "CDx3 Preferred Stocks" regular preferred stocks must meet the ten CDx3 Selection Criteria presented in chapter 7. For example:

1) The issuing company must have a *perfect track record* of never having suspended dividends on a preferred stock, and remember these are multi-billion dollar decades-old companies;

2) The dividends must be *'cumulative'* meaning that if the issuing company misses a dividend payment to you they have to make it up to you later (they still owe you the money); and

3) Carry an *investment grade* Moody's creditworthiness rating.

Part III: Buying When The Market Favors Buyers

CDx3 Investors always purchase their CDx3 Preferred Stocks when the market price tends to be below $25 per share. Chapters 9, 10 and 11 will teach you how to do this, but remember that the $25 share price becomes very important throughout the discussion.

Depending on market conditions, buyers will either be buying new preferred stocks or older issues using something called the CDx3 Bargain Table, a technique for identifying bargains at just the right time. Either way, the result is the same – you will be purchasing your CDx3 Preferred Stocks for less than $25 per share.

Part IV: Selling When The Market Favors Sellers

You will have two specific opportunities to sell your CDx3 Preferred Stock for a capital gain (if you so choose). And you will know about them way in advance – at least months if not longer, right down to the day.

How can that be?

Since CDx3 Investors always purchase their CDx3 Preferred Stocks for less than $25 per share, earning a capital gain downstream is all about knowing when the market price of your CDx3 Preferred Stock is likely to climb to $25 per share or higher.

But how do you know if you are better off by selling today or holding onto your CDx3 Preferred Stock a little longer and collecting more dividend payments?

Chapter 13 shows you the Target Sell Price calculation – during a seller's market, if the market price exceeds the Target Sell Price of your CDx3 Preferred Stock you should consider selling.

By using the Target Sell Price as a guide, the guesswork and emotion of making selling decisions is eliminated for you.

You will also learn about the "built-in buyer" of your CDx3 Preferred Stocks. If you decide not to sell for your Target Sell Price, every CDx3 Preferred Stock has a built-in buyer in the form of the issuing company itself who may purchase your shares back from you for $25 per share at a specific future point in time.

Chapter 14 describes this built-in buyer and how you can determine if they are likely to purchase your CDx3 Preferred Stock shares back from you downstream.

Whether you sell your shares for a market price at, or above, the Target Sell Price or hold your shares, collecting more dividend income, and sell to your built-in buyer downstream, the CDx3 Income Engine provides CDx3 Investors with multiple capital gain opportunities (should you decide to sell).

Part V: Building Your CDx3 Portfolio

After you learn how to screen, buy and sell the highest quality preferred stocks – CDx3 Preferred Stocks – you will have a decision to make. Do you want to build your personal CDx3 Portfolio yourself or would you rather the CDx3 Notification Service do the research and calculations for you?

Throughout this book, and summarized again in Appendix A, I will provide you with the resources that you will need to be a successful CDx3 Investor on your own. Most of the resources that you will need are not only readily available, but are free to anyone who knows how to use their web browser.

For those who would rather someone else do the research and calculations and simply receive an email message when there are buying or selling opportunities, I offer the CDx3 Notification Service.

Chapter 18 shows you some of the resources that subscribers to the CDx3 Notification Service have available to them and how they are used to build a CDx3 Portfolio with almost no work at all since it is all done for you. You can even take a tour of the subscriber's exclusive website and see the screens for yourself.

Part V provides some very valuable tips regarding how to jump start your CDx3 Portfolio and how to determine when it will reach a magic milestone when it is generating enough dividend income to fund your next purchase entirely on its own without any "new" money from you.

And chapter 19 walks you through the mechanics of setting your bid price and placing your first CDx3 Preferred Stock buy order using an online trading account.

Now let's get to it. It's time to learn about preferred stock investing using the CDx3 Income Engine.

PART I

The Preferred Stock Market

Thank you for a wonderful service and your outstanding insight into a greatly under-covered corner of the investment universe!
- Jonathan S.

Thanks to you I'm (finally) having fun in the stock market.
- John F.

It is important to understand a few things about the preferred stock market itself.

As you are about to see, knowing a few basic characteristics of CDx3 Preferred Stocks, and the forces that drive their market prices, is essential for taking advantage of various economic conditions. Specifically:

- ✓ Chapter 1 explains why the CDx3 Income Engine uses high quality preferred stocks to achieve its objectives (maximize revenue while minimizing risk and work) rather than some other type of investment (such as bonds, CDs or common stocks);

- ✓ Chapter 2 describes the three different types of preferred stocks and how they come to market;

- ✓ Chapter 3 presents how the Three Rules Of Market Price Predictability move the market price of CDx3 Preferred Stocks;

- ✓ Chapter 4 uses the Global Credit Crisis to illustrate the performance of the CDx3 Income Engine under the most extreme conditions; and

- ✓ Chapter 5 provides a method for observing the marketplace for CDx3 Preferred Stocks. By that I mean its strength (or lack thereof), direction and magnitude of its changes. And do so with information provided by others for free.

WHY PREFERRED STOCKS?

Preferred stocks are one of the most, if not the most, underused and misunderstood investments available to individual investors.

There is nothing complicated about preferred stocks. You buy and sell them using unique trading symbols much like other investments such as common stocks or bonds. And they pay you a periodic (quarterly) dividend that is of a fixed amount much like a certificate of deposit from your local bank (monthly).

But before explaining the difference between preferred stocks, common stocks, bonds and bank CDs let me shed some light on what a preferred stock is.

Preferred Stock – Why The Fancy Name?

Throughout this book I refer to "CDx3 Preferred Stocks." A CDx3 Preferred Stock is a regular preferred stock that meets the ten selection criteria described in chapter 7.

Preferred stocks have been around for many years. In fact, there are still several preferred stocks trading that were issued during the 1930s (Consolidated Edison, ED-A, 5.00%, March 24, 1936).

Originally, and for several decades, preferred stocks were primarily sold by utilities. Although many still think of them as being issued by utilities alone, that has not actually been the case since the early 1990s. Today all kinds of companies issue preferred stocks.

To raise money companies can either (1) borrow money or (2) sell off part of their company in the form of common stock shares or preferred stock shares. Either way, there is a cost associated with raising cash - the "cost of money."

Interest Versus Dividends

When you buy a bond, you are essentially loaning the company cash in exchange for a return in the form of interest and a promise saying that, at some future point, they will give you your principal back.

Their obligation to pay you back shows up on the company's balance sheet as "debt" like any other loan. The company is now indebted to you along with their other lenders. The company is allowed to deduct the interest payments to you off of their taxes as a cost of doing business.

When you buy a share of a company's *common* stock there is no promise whatsoever of any future return. Nor is there any obligation to pay you any type of return.

If the company does well and is profitable, a portion of those profits may be shared with you, or not, as determined by the company's board of directors.

Since purchasers of a company's common stock are paid their return, if any, out of the company's profits (according to how many shares you own), and these payments are at risk depending upon how well the company does, you are considered to be one of the company's owners; you have an "equity" position in the company.

The return, if any, that you realize on your shares of common stock is a dividend rather than interest.

Where interest is a business expense as the cost of borrowing money on a loan, dividends are paid out of profits to owners. So where bond investors receive and pay taxes on *interest* payments from the company, common stockholders receive and pay taxes on *dividend* income.

Since the tax treatment of interest and dividend income is different, there may be a tax difference to you by investing in bonds versus common stocks. Your tax advisor should be able to guide you on this point.

Now To Preferred Stocks

Preferred stocks have a unique trading symbol and trade on the New York Stock Exchange (NYSE), so you buy them just as you would a common stock (more on preferred stock trading symbols in a moment).

A given company can have several "series" of preferred stocks trading at any time; that is, over time, as the company needs cash for various projects it can issue a preferred stock series (series A, B, C, etc.). Each series is described in an accompanying document called a "prospectus."[1]

The prospectus spells out the obligations that the issuing company has to investors who purchase a share of that series preferred stock, such as the dividend rate that will be paid to you, the payment schedule and much more.

When you purchase a share of a company's preferred stock you are considered to be an owner – you have "equity" in the issuing company.

---

[1] See Appendix B: CDx3 Special Report "*Prospectus For The Rest Of Us*"

But unlike common stock, preferred stocks pay a fixed periodic dividend to you. You are going to receive the same dividend amount every period[2]. It does not fluctuate, so you know, in advance, what your payments are going to be (although there is such a thing as a variable rate preferred stock but these are rare). Consequently, preferred stocks are seen as lower risk than the same company's common stock.

Further, if the company is running low on cash and does not have enough to pay the dividends to both its common and preferred stock shareholders, those holding the preferred stock shares get paid first and in full before common stockholder see a dime – you have preferred status; hence the name "preferred stock."

Preferred stock dividends, being known in advance, are therefore more related to a company's *cash flow* than to this quarter's *profits*.

What do you give up with preferred stock?

In exchange for the lower risk, fixed known dividend payments and getting to stand in line in front of common stockholders, preferred stockholders must give up their voting rights. That means that you will not be asked to vote in corporate elections or on company policy decisions.

But let's face it – unless you own hundreds of thousands or even millions of shares, no one in any corporate boardroom is waiting breathlessly for your ballot to arrive.

For most of us, giving up voting rights in exchange for the benefits of preferred stocks is a no-brainer.

So now you have a basic idea of the difference between bonds, common stock and preferred stock.

---

[2] See Appendix B: CDx3 Special Report "*Dividend Accounting*"

Certificates Of Deposit (CDs)

Another fixed-income investment alternative for individual investors is certificates of deposits (CDs) that you buy at your local bank. Let me say up front that I am not a fan of CDs for a variety of reasons, the biggest reason being that you cannot make any real money investing in a bank CD.

You are told that you can make good money by flashy advertisements, but some pretty simple math makes it clear that this is just not the case and it never has been.

As I showed you in the Forward to this book, by the time you subtract off inflation and the income taxes on the interest that CDs pay your actual gain is little or nothing.

While bank CDs may be an appropriate place to temporarily store some cash that you will be needing shortly, I hesitate to call them an investment.

Side-By-Side Comparison

The U.S. economy is bigger than the next three world economies combined (including China, Japan and Germany)[3]. With all of the investment opportunities that the U.S. economy offers us, it just seems to me that individual investors should be able to earn a respectable return at acceptable risk.

By comparing some of the key investment features of bank CDs, bonds, common stocks and preferred stocks you will be able to see why I feel that preferred stocks can offer a spectacular investment alternative for individual investors, brokers and their clients and investment groups.

---

[3] Source: *The World Bank,* worldbank.org. Based on 2010 GDP

First, in order to earn an effective annual return north of 10%, which is what the CDx3 Income Engine is tuned to do, you are going to need more than just a single stream of interest or dividend income.

Interest rates from bank CDs and bonds and dividend rates paid by common stocks and preferred stocks are rarely above 10%. Depending on economic conditions, CDs, bonds and common stocks will pay less than 6% (although there are a few exceptions) and investment grade preferred stocks pay between 6% and 9% (with one exception at 9.6%).

So we know from the start that in order to earn more than 10% annually, we are going to need more than just dividend income.

Specifically, we are going to need two income streams: fixed periodic income plus the ability to sell the investment downstream for more than we originally paid, adding that profit (called a "capital gain") to the fixed periodic income that we have been earning along the way.

By adding a downstream capital gain to our fixed periodic income we stand a pretty good chance of getting over the 10% bar.

The following table compares the income streams produced by bank CDs, bonds, common stocks and preferred stocks. A quick look at the table makes it pretty clear why the CDx3 Income Engine uses preferred stocks.

Income Stream	Bank CDs	Bonds	Common Stocks	Preferred Stocks
Fixed Periodic Income	Yes	Yes	No	Yes
Capital Gain Income Opportunity	No	Yes	Yes	Yes
Receive Income For Full Period	Yes	No	Yes	Yes

While bank CDs generate fixed periodic (monthly) interest income, they offer no opportunity for a capital gain whatsoever; in fact, as I presented in the Forward, the value of your original investment will often be lower when you get your principal back from the bank than it was originally (after subtracting inflation).

And with bonds, you do not get to keep all of the interest they earn. While you may earn a capital gain when you sell your bond, you do not get to keep all of the interest income from the first or last period of your ownership.

Bonds usually pay your interest payment to you every six months. But you only get to keep the amount of that interest for your time of ownership. For example, if you buy a bond two months into its six month payment period, you will receive four months worth of the interest for that period (which is accounted for in the price you pay) while the person who sold the bond to you will get to keep two months worth of interest.

While this might make sense and seem perfectly fair to those who buy bonds, it is totally unreasonable to preferred stock investors.

Why? Because when you buy a share of a preferred stock, *you get to keep the entire dividend quarter's worth of dividend income regardless of how many days during the dividend quarter you owned it.*

There is no proration with preferred stocks.

That's right. You could own a preferred stock for just one day and you will receive 90 days worth of dividend income and you get to keep all of it[4].

Further, as you can see in the above table, preferred stocks also offer the opportunity for a downstream capital gain. And in the coming

---

[4] See Appendix B: CDx3 Special Report *"Who Gets The Money"*

chapters I am going to teach you the Three Rules of Market Price Predictability that help you to capture it.

Preferred stocks pay a fixed dividend well above that being paid by competing bank CDs, offer the opportunity for a great capital gain on top of that dividend income and do so at acceptable risk – if you know how to identify the highest quality preferreds, which you will be learning momentarily.

Combining the two income streams – fixed periodic dividends plus a downstream capital gain – does the trick as you can see by the chart on the back cover of this book and as itemized for you in chapter 15.

What I Really Like About Preferred Stocks

The double dose of income - dividend income now plus capital gain income downstream – that can be earned by investing in the highest quality preferred stocks - CDx3 Preferred Stocks - is just the beginning of what I really like about them.

The more I research CDx3 Preferred Stocks, the more aspects of them I find that are pretty easy to warm up to.

And I'm not talking about the obvious things like above average dividend income, monthly income generation or the great dividend track record. As you will see later, you get all of those characteristics with CDx3 Preferred Stocks automatically as well.

I'm talking about other details and mechanics that make CDx3 Preferred Stocks very easy to like.

Early Warning System

Wouldn't it be great if you had a light mounted on your wall that would start flashing if there was something risky going on with one of your preferred stocks?

CDx3 Preferred Stocks have a built-in "early warning system" that lets you know in advance if your "pay-attention" light should be flashing.

Remember why they are called "preferred stocks." Preferred stockholders get paid our dividends each quarter prior to common stockholders.

Every quarter, companies that issue CDx3 Preferred Stocks have to announce whether or not they have enough cash to pay the upcoming dividends to holders of their *common* stock.

When doing so, the company may increase their common stock dividend, decrease it, eliminate it entirely or leave it the same. As long as the issuing company pays a *common* stock dividend, even if it is $0.0000001 per share, you, as a *preferred* stockholder, know that you are going be getting paid your full dividend amount.

In other words, as long as common stockholders are going to be getting paid (any amount at all), preferred stockholders, by law, are going to be getting paid first and in full.

So the common stock dividend announcements that company's make act as an early warning system for preferred stock shareholders.

Companies make these announcements every quarter a few weeks before the dividends actually get paid. So, if you find yourself concerned about your next preferred stock dividend payment, just keep an eye on the company's *common* stock dividend announcements.

These announcements are made with the quarterly financial reports that are filed with the Securities and Exchange Commission (SEC) and the schedule for upcoming announcements is generally posted on the company's website under Investor Relations.

Dividends Based On Your Number Of Shares

This point is especially important to remember: preferred stock investors are paid *based on the number of shares you own*, not the then-current market price and not on your original purchase price.

When your dividends are calculated, the issuing company multiplies the declared dividend rate by a fixed dollar amount (not the current market price nor your purchase price) called the "par value."

In the case of CDx3 Preferred Stocks this fixed dollar amount is $25.00. For example, a CDx3 Preferred Stock that has a declared dividend rate of 8% is going to pay you $2.00 per year in dividend income *for every share that you own* (8% x $25) *regardless of the market price.*

Current market price is *irrelevant* to your dividend income; it's all about how many shares you own.

Unlike common stock investors, savvy preferred stock investors savor, rather than fear, a period of falling market prices. When shares become relatively cheap, it is time to accumulate more of them for bargain prices and build your portfolio of dividend-paying shares.

The point bears repeating – with preferred stocks you are paid *based on the number of shares you own*, not the then-current market price. While common stock investors, looking for a big run up in value (buy low, sell high) are staking their fortunes on market price behavior, preferred stock investors seek to accumulate more shares.

Do not fall into the trap of using *common* stock investing metrics to evaluate the success of your *preferred* stock investment.

Buy For Less Than $25 And Boost Your Yield

As described above, preferred stock dividends are calculated using a fixed par value ($25 per share in our case). In other words, you get paid as if you have purchased your shares for $25.00 each, whether or not you actually have.

What that means is that if you can figure out a way to purchase your CDx3 Preferred Stocks for a price less than $25.00 per share (which I am about to teach you how to do), you are actually making more than the declared dividend rate (8% in our above example).

The return on the money you actually have invested (your "yield") is actually higher than the declared dividend rate when you purchase your shares for less than $25.00 each. So then it's just a matter of finding CDx3 Preferred Stocks that are available for a market price below $25.

Take a look at this table.

Your Purchase Price	Declared Dividend Rate						
	6.50%	6.75%	7.00%	7.25%	7.50%	7.75%	8.00%
$25.00	6.50%	6.75%	7.00%	7.25%	7.50%	7.75%	8.00%
$24.75	6.57%	6.82%	7.07%	7.32%	7.58%	7.83%	8.08%
$24.50	6.63%	6.89%	7.14%	7.40%	7.65%	7.91%	8.16%
$24.25	6.70%	6.96%	7.22%	7.47%	7.73%	7.99%	8.25%
$24.00	6.77%	7.03%	7.29%	7.55%	7.81%	8.07%	8.33%
$23.75	6.84%	7.11%	7.37%	7.63%	7.89%	8.16%	8.42%
$23.50	6.91%	7.18%	7.45%	7.71%	7.98%	8.24%	8.51%
$23.25	6.99%	7.26%	7.53%	7.80%	8.06%	8.33%	8.60%
$23.00	7.07%	7.34%	7.61%	7.88%	8.15%	8.42%	8.70%
$22.75	7.14%	7.42%	7.69%	7.97%	8.24%	8.52%	8.79%
$22.50	7.22%	7.50%	7.78%	8.06%	8.33%	8.61%	8.89%
$22.25	7.30%	7.58%	7.87%	8.15%	8.43%	8.71%	8.99%
$22.00	7.39%	7.67%	7.95%	8.24%	8.52%	8.81%	9.09%
$21.75	7.47%	7.76%	8.05%	8.33%	8.62%	8.91%	9.20%
$21.50	7.56%	7.85%	8.14%	8.43%	8.72%	9.01%	9.30%
$21.25	7.65%	7.94%	8.24%	8.53%	8.82%	9.12%	9.41%
$21.00	7.74%	8.04%	8.33%	8.63%	8.93%	9.23%	9.52%

Notice that for every dollar below $25 that you purchase your CDx3 Preferred Stocks for, your actual yield will jump up between 0.25% and 0.50%. And if you can find a way to purchase a share of your 8% CDx3 Preferred Stock for $21, your dividend yield goes up by over 1.5%, jumping to 9.52%.

Market Price Predictability

Another aspect of preferred stocks that I really like is that there are many more "knowns" than with common stocks and we're going to use that fact to our advantage in the coming chapters.

This is especially true when it comes to the predictability of the market price of CDx3 Preferred Stocks.

It's not that you will know what the market price is going to do on any given day. That requires clairvoyance which is always in incredibly short supply.

But, short of being clairvoyant, there are short-term, longer-term and "end-term" aspects to the market price behavior of CDx3 Preferred Stocks that make common stock investing look like little more than throwing darts at a dart board.

Seems like a bold statement, and I guess it is. After all, you're probably not used to the words "market price" and "predictable" appearing in the same sentence within an investing book. Being able to predict (within a certain margin of error) what the market price of an investment is going to be on a specific date in the future seems like a hunt for the fountain of youth.

But like Galileo once said "all truths are easy to understand, once they are discovered."

So now you know what a preferred stock is and why the CDx3 Income Engine uses high quality preferred stocks, rather than some other form of investment, to achieve its three objectives – maximize revenue while minimizing risk and work.

For the remainder of this Part of *Preferred Stock Investing*, I will explain how a new preferred stock is created (this can become important when you are looking to buy a preferred stock) and the Three Rules of Market Price Predictability that drive the market price of CDx3 Preferred Stocks in specific ways and at specific times.

Once you understand how the market price of CDx3 Preferred Stocks tends to move at different periods of time and under different market conditions, I will conclude this Part by showing you how the market prices for CDx3 Preferred Stocks during the extreme conditions of the Global Credit Crisis behaved exactly the way the Three Rules of Market Price Predictability said they would.

You see, the Three Rules of Market Price Predictability (chapter 3) and how they integrate with the ten CDx3 Selection Criteria (chapter 7) are designed such that the *reasons* behind market conditions are irrelevant. Whether a buyer's market or seller's market is being caused by uncertainty related to war (2002), a housing bubble (2005/06), a Global Credit Crisis (2007 – 2009) or recession (2010+), the CDx3 Income Engine works the same way.

CREATING A NEW PREFERRED STOCK

The task of creating a new CDx3 Preferred Stock involves a sequence of steps executed in a very specific order by a myriad of organizations both public and private.

As a CDx3 Investor, this sequence of events is important to you since, as you will learn in Part III, there comes a point when a new CDx3 Preferred Stock is generally available at a substantial discount.

While we will not get into the reasons why this occurs just yet, suffice it to say that knowing when it occurs can become a very important piece of information.

Before diving into the sequence of events that ultimately leads to a new CDx3 Preferred Stock hitting the market for your consideration, I want to provide you with a brief summary of the three types of preferred stocks. One of these three types – trust preferred stocks – offers a specific opportunity to preferred stock investors under the 2010 Wall Street Reform Act that you should be sure to read about.

Every CDx3 Preferred Stock that you add to your CDx3 Portfolio will be one of these three types.

Types Of Preferred Stocks

There are three types of preferred stocks – traditional preferreds, trust preferreds and third-party trust preferreds. While the attributes of these three types – cumulative, convertible, mandatory convertible, variable or fixed-rate – can vary, there are just three types.

The distinction between them has tax treatment consequences to the issuing company, but to the CDx3 Investor the distinction is largely irrelevant and the dividend income is all the same. But, for those who intend on wading through the provisions of the prospectus language[1], knowing the difference between them may clear a few things up.

Let's take them one at a time.

Traditional Preferred Stocks

Prior to the early 1990s traditional preferred stocks were primarily issued by utilities. Since then, however, many different kinds of companies have seen the light.

Today, in addition to utilities, traditional preferred stocks are issued by companies with an interest in apartments, shopping centers, self-storage, medical facilities, shipping logistics centers, hotels, office buildings, insurance companies, banks and brokerage firms.

Dividends that are paid to you by traditional preferred stock, being dividends rather than interest, are not tax deductible for the issuing company.

Some traditional preferred stocks are eligible for special 15% tax treatment as specified by the 2003 Tax Relief Act, although qualifying issues usually come with more investment risk.

---

[1] It is always a good idea to review the prospectus before investing. For tips regarding how to simplify this chore see Appendix B, CDx3 Special Report *"Prospectus For The Rest Of Us."*

Let me show you what I mean. In an analysis of the 96 traditional preferred stocks issued during 2007 and 2010 that qualified for the 15% tax treatment under the Act, none are able to meet the ten CDx3 Selection Criteria.

Of these 96 tax advantaged traditional preferreds only 55 carried an "investment grade" credit rating from Moody's (CDx3 Selection Criteria number 4). Of these remaining 55 only 34 were issued by U.S. companies (CDx3 Selection Criteria number 7); and of these 34 only four had the "cumulative" dividend requirement (CDx3 Selection Criteria number 6).

And only one of these paid a dividend of 6.5% or higher (CDx3 Selection Criteria number 1; we'll learn much more about the CDx3 Selection Criteria in chapter 7).

The one remaining 15% issue is the Series A traditional preferred stock issued by Gabelli Global Gold, Natural Resources and Income Fund (AMEX: GGN-A). Note that GGN-A does not qualify as a CDx3 Preferred Stock since by purchasing GGN-A shares you are actually buying shares in a specific non-diversified investment fund, not a company. And dividends from GGN-A are conditional upon the continuation of a Aaa rating by Moody's of the fund (a specific investment grade sub-category).

From this analysis it seems that to get the 15% tax treatment on traditional preferred stocks, you're going to be investing primarily in speculative grade, non-cumulative preferreds issued by foreign companies that pay a relatively low dividend rate.

For most CDx3 Investors, any savings from the 15% tax rate is overcome by the additional risk and low dividend payments. The CDx3 Income Engine favors lower risk over lower taxes.

Trust Preferred Stocks

The 2010 Wall Street Reform Act created an opportunity for preferred stock investors involving trust preferred stocks (TRUPS) that I will describe in a moment, but first let's be sure we understand what they are.

I mentioned in the Introduction that when a company pays *interest* (on a loan or other form of debt) that interest is tax deductible off of the issuing company's taxes.

But *dividends* paid to stockholders, including the company's preferred stockholders, are a distribution of profits and are therefore not tax deductable to the issuing company. Interest payments are tax deductible, dividend payments are not.

Trust preferred stocks involve a bit of Wall Street sleight of hand that leaves the issuing company in a position whereby they are able to deduct the cost of your dividends, hence delivering a tax advantage to the issuing company.

This maneuver is transparent to you, the investor. When a company wants to issue a trust preferred stock the issuing company sets up a separate company called a trust. The trust issues a preferred stock to the marketplace (which you buy) generating cash for the trust.

The trust loans the issuing company that cash in exchange for debt notes (a loan). The company pays interest on this loan to the trust which the trust, in turn, uses to pay your dividends.

Notice by this structure the issuing company is paying interest (to the trust) which is tax deductible. You receive your dividends from the trust so you don't know or care about the difference.

The net result is that the issuing company is able to turn your *dividend* payments into a tax deduction. Nice trick. Remember though that the trust receives interest from the issuing company which the trust is obligated to pay income tax on. But, with a trust preferred stock, the burden of doing so is passed from the issuing company to the trust.

TRUPS are issued primarily by banks but not because the banks are necessarily desperate for a tax deduction. Banks issue TRUPS because the capital raised by doing so counts toward a key measure of the bank's reserves that regulators call "Tier 1 Capital." Banks are required to meet certain minimum levels of Tier 1 Capital and by issuing TRUPS most banks are able to stay on the good side of these regulators.

Section 171 of the 2010 Wall Street Reform Act includes a provision that, beginning January 1, 2013, Big Banks (assets greater than $15 billion) will no longer be able to count the value of their TRUPS toward Tier 1 Capital. This provision removes the primary reason that Big Banks issued these TRUPS to begin with.

Since the main benefit has been removed, the likelihood that these Big Bank TRUPS will be retired ("called") goes up substantially. Upon a call, whoever owns shares will receive $25.00 per share. Several Big Bank TRUPS not only meet all ten of the CDx3 Selection Criteria, but are also available for a market price less than $25.00. Purchasing a Big Bank TRUPS for less than $25 now positions you for not only the great dividend income these securities provide but also positions you for a capital gain in the event of a call. Thanks to the U.S. government[2].

Third-Party Trust Preferred Stock

As a CDx3 Investor, it is unlikely that you will see many third-party trust preferred stocks. Third-party trust preferreds are similar to trust preferreds in that they involve the creation of a trust company from whom you actually purchase your preferred stock shares.

---

[2] Taking advantage of the Big Bank TRUPS opportunity created by the 2010 Wall Street Reform Act is discussed in detail in chapter 10.

But where trust preferreds are structured to provide a tax benefit to the issuing company, a third-party trust preferred is created for the sole purpose of generating a profit to the issuing company (usually a brokerage firm).

The brokerage firm (the first party) sets up a trust company from whom you (the second party) are going to be buying preferred stock. The brokerage firm then buys high quality preferred stocks or debt securities (like bonds) issued by another company (the third party) on the open market. These securities are sold to the trust as backing for preferred stock that the trust issues to you, the investor (at a mark up over the original open market cost).

This structure is little more than a mechanism for a brokerage company to buy high quality preferred stocks at retail (on the open market that you have access to as well as they do) and resell them to you at a higher price.

Setting The Declared Dividend Rate

Once the issuing company decides what type of preferred stock (traditional, trust or third-party trust) to bring to market they move on to drafting up the prospectus which, of course, includes the task of setting the declared dividend rate.

While it may seem a bit counterintuitive, the issuing company does not set the declared dividend rate. Rather, the declared dividend rate is identified by a group of investment bankers referred to as the "underwriters."

The underwriters are the ones who actually purchase the new preferred shares from the issuing company; the issuing company gets cash, the underwriters get the new preferred stock shares.

The underwriters turn right around and sell these shares to brokers ("dealers") who, in turn, sell them to you in response to any buy order that you have placed with them.

The underwriters do not want to ever get stuck with the shares that they purchased from the issuing company. So the underwriters need to know, for a fact and in advance, that the dealer/brokers are going to buy the shares from them.

The dealer/brokers, of course, feel the same way. They need to know that investors (including large pension funds, large companies and individual investors like you) are going to buy the shares as well.

In other words, starting with the underwriters, there needs to be confirmation that there is demand in the market for the issuing company's preferred stock shares before the shares are actually issued.

So the question to the underwriters becomes "what dividend rate do these preferred shares have to pay for 'The Market' to buy them at $25.00 per share?"

Many factors go into this analysis, but the underwriters ultimately come back to the issuing company and agree to purchase the new preferred stock shares. But only if the issuing company is willing to set the declared dividend rate that the underwriters have determined The Market will accept (i.e. that there is demand for in the marketplace) at $25 per share.

Once the issuing company and the underwriters agree on the declared dividend rate for the new preferred stock issue, the prospectus is finalized and filed with the SEC.

Three Steps To Market

With a few exceptions, once the prospectus is filed with the SEC the new preferred stock issue goes through three more steps:

1) Obtain regulatory approval and credit agency rating. If you are a subscriber to the CDx3 Notification Service, it is at this step that you receive the "just announced" email message. The issuing company receives the underwriter's cash at this time. This is the official Initial Public Offering (IPO) date, even though the shares are not yet available to the general public; then

2) Begin public trading on the Over-The-Counter (OTC) stock exchange[3], usually at very favorable pricing, under a temporary trading symbol (more on this in a moment). For subscribers, this step triggers the "now trading" email alert that you receive; then

3) Transfer trading to the New York Stock Exchange (NYSE) under the permanent trading symbol once the trading application is approved by the NYSE. This is when subscribers receive the "X becomes Y" email message notifying them of the change of trading symbol.

Your local broker usually becomes aware of a new preferred stock once its trading application has been approved by the NYSE at step 3.

By following the instructions in chapter 9 (or by subscribing to the CDx3 Notification Service) you will usually be aware of new preferred stocks well before your local broker knows about them.

Preferred Stock Trading Symbols

When buying and selling CDx3 Preferred Stocks you need to know how the financial services industry denotes preferred stock trading symbols.

---

[3] See Appendix B: CDx3 Special Report *"Trading Over-The-Counter"*

The methods currently used to identify a preferred stock are the result of automating a system that was designed long ago, in a non-automated world.

Temporary Trading Symbols

On the previous page I pointed out that new CDx3 Preferred Stocks will usually begin public trading on what is called the Over-The-Counter stock exchange (OTC) while waiting for the NYSE to approve the trading application.

In chapter 9 you will learn all about the OTC, how it works for you as a preferred stock investor and when to use it to your financial advantage.

When a new CDx3 Preferred Stock becomes available for purchase on the OTC it is provided with a temporary trading symbol, usually (but not always) five characters in length.

The Series P CDx3 Preferred Stock introduced by Public Storage, Inc. on October 4, 2010, for example, traded on the OTC under the temporary trading symbol PSAPL for six days prior to its transfer to the NYSE where its permanent symbol became PSA-P. Your broker automatically transfers any shares of PSAPL that you may have purchased on the OTC and PSA-P shows as the new trading symbol on your statement.

Permanent Trading Symbols

The trading symbol for a *common* stock is the same regardless of which online service you use to reference the stock. International Business Machines, for example, is referenced by the symbol "IBM" regardless if you are using TDAmeritrade, Yahoo! Finance or MarketWatch.

Unfortunately, this is not the case with preferred stocks. There are several standards for the trading symbols of preferred stocks depending on which online service you are using. So, if you type a preferred stock symbol into an online service and get an "invalid symbol" message, try one of the other naming conventions that I describe here.

Let's take an example where Public Storage Inc. introduces a new preferred stock. Since companies can introduce several issues of new preferred stocks in a very short period of time, the financial services industry, for the most part, has settled on the convention of identifying each issue with a sequential letter designation. The first issue would be identified as series A, the second issue would be identified as series B and so on.

Public Storage's common stock trades on the New York Stock Exchange under the symbol PSA. When Public Storage introduced their first preferred stock issue, it was identified by the following symbols, depending on the service you were querying:

	Online Service	Preferred Stock Symbol Convention
1	TDAmeritrade, Google Finance and throughout this book	PSA-A
2	Yahoo Finance and others	PSA-PA
3	NYSE, MarketWatch (see also #7), Fidelity and others	PSAPRA
4	E*Trade	PSA.PR.A
5	Schwab	PSA+A
6	Scottrade[4]	PSApA
7	MarketWatch (see also #3)	PSA.PRA

---

[4] Portions of Scottrade's system have trouble with preferred stock symbols entered as all uppercase characters. Using a lowercase 'p' to denote a preferred issue seems to work best with Scottrade.

Throughout this book I use the hyphen convention so the series A CDx3 Preferred Stock from Public Storage is referred to as PSA-A here.

In the second case, a "P" is inserted after the hyphen. In the third case, the letters "PR" replace the hyphen. In the fourth case, the hyphen is replaced with ".PR." The fifth convention, used by Schwab, replaced the hyphen with a plus sign. In the case of Scottrade, the letter "p" replaces the hyphen. And lastly, if you are having trouble with MarketWatch accepting the PR convention seen in #3, there are portions of the MarketWatch system that use the letters ".PR" in place of the hyphen.

You may want to earmark this table. If you are a new preferred stock investor you will understand the value of this table when you go to enter your first buy order.

THREE

THE THREE RULES OF MARKET PRICE PREDICTABILITY

One of the many very appealing aspects of preferred stock investing is that with preferred stocks that meet the ten CDx3 Selection Criteria you know an enormous amount about the behavior of their market price at various points in time.

There is nothing predictable about the future pricing of common stocks. With CDx3 Preferred Stocks, however, there is a great deal of predictability. Predictability that, when you understand it, provides CDx3 Investors with a respectable return at acceptable risk.

Unlike common stocks, CDx3 Preferred Stocks (which, again, are regular preferred stocks that meet the ten selection criteria from chapter 7) have to play by certain rules which I'll describe in a moment. Common stocks, on the other hand, are completely freewheeling. Their market price at any point in time depends completely on the moods and decisions of buyers and sellers and is therefore subject to often dramatic jumps from one day to the next.

While the daily market prices of CDx3 Preferred Stocks change as well, the forces that act upon them are very different from the forces that act upon common stocks. The market price of a CDx3 Preferred Stock is heavily influenced by three specific rules:

1) The Rule of Buyer/Seller Behavior;

2) The Rule of Rate/Price Opposition; and

3) The Rule of Call Date Gravity.

The first of these rules, the Rule of Buyer/Seller Behavior, influences the market price of a CDx3 Preferred Stock during the short-term of a given dividend quarter.

The Rule of Rate/Price Opposition pressures the market price of a CDx3 Preferred Stock for its entire life span until the Rule of Call Date Gravity kicks in (much more on this later).

The third rule, the Rule of Call Date Gravity, explains distortion in the market price of a CDx3 Preferred Stock that can occur once the security becomes "callable" by the issuing company. We'll be learning much more about how to take advantage of the call date in chapter 14.

These three rules work in harmony to influence the market price of CDx3 Preferred Stocks in a manner that is predictable enough to allow you to purchase shares at a time that tends to favor buyers and, if you're a seller, determine the price you are going to sell your CDx3 Preferred Stock shares for and when, the specific date, that price is most likely to occur.

And the best part is that, since you will know the date that your "Target Sell Price" (discussed in chapter 13) is most likely to occur, there is no point in checking the price every day. By using the CDx3 Income Engine approach, there is nothing to do the rest of the time; just check the market price of your CDx3 Preferred Stock one day each quarter, a day that you will know way in advance – that's all there is to it.

Rule #1: The Rule Of Buyer/Seller Behavior

If I name a CDx3 Preferred Stock, could you tell me what the market price is *most likely* to be three months from now?

If not, you will be able to in just a couple of minutes.

Notice that I said "...most likely..." There can always be outside influences that distort the results away from what an otherwise perfect market would do.

Fortunately, as we will discuss at length in chapter 5 we can measure that distortion and make adjustments accordingly. But for now let's talk about the generic case.

Buyers and sellers of any type of dividend paying investment have three behaviors in common:

1) All buyers of CDx3 Preferred Stocks (as well as buyers of any other kind of investment) want the same thing – the lowest price;

2) And all sellers of CDx3 Preferred Stocks want the same thing – the highest price; and

3) Buyers and sellers would rather receive their dividend cash sooner rather than later (if I offered you $100 today or the same $100 three months from now, which would you pick?).

Because CDx3 Selection Criteria number 3 (discussed in chapter 7) requires that CDx3 Preferred Stocks pay their dividends quarterly, these three predictable behaviors of buyers and sellers influence the market price of CDx3 Preferred Stocks in a predictable way – the Rule of Buyer/Seller Behavior - within any given dividend quarter.

Wouldn't it be great if you could put the buyers and sellers together and watch the buyers try to outbid one another on a CDx3 Preferred Stock that you owned, raising the price higher and higher? And wouldn't it be even greater if you knew *in advance* when – the exact date – that they were going to reach this "highest bid" maximum price?

If you knew when buyers and sellers were going to reach such an agreement on the price of a CDx3 Preferred Stock that you owned – and you knew it in advance – you wouldn't even have to watch the bidding day in and day out; you'd just need to show up on the date when the price peaks and collect your profits. It wouldn't really matter what went on the rest of the time.

Much of the time, with CDx3 Preferred Stocks, you can do exactly that. The predictable nature of the behavior of buyers and sellers converges with a legal requirement (that I will discuss later in this chapter) and tends to elevate the market price of your CDx3 Preferred Stock over the course of a dividend quarter.

We're Only Human

Let's say you buy a share of a CDx3 Preferred Stock for $25.00 on the first day it is available for public purchase. And let's say the declared dividend rate on your CDx3 Preferred Stock is 8.0%. That's $2.00 per year or $0.50 per quarter in dividend income to you.

You're now sitting there tapping your toe, trying to stay calm in anticipation of receiving your first dividend payment.

The closer you get to the end of the first quarter, the more excited you get.

Finally, you are one day away from "payday." The day before you're going to make a cool five dimes, I give you a call and offer you $25.30 for your share.

Remember, the dividend you are going to receive the very next day is $0.50 so you'll be up $0.50 if you wait until tomorrow.

Why would you sell your share to me the day before and lose out on the much anticipated dividend that you are going to be receiving the very next day (not to mention all future dividends thereafter)?

Answer: you wouldn't; and neither would anyone else.

In fact, you would make it clear to me that you would not sell your share to me for any less than, say, $25.49 (getting your money one day early is apparently worth a penny to you).

In the financial services industry, the date when it is determined who gets the upcoming quarterly dividend payment is called the "ex-dividend date." If the stock trading public was allowed to name this date they would have probably called it the "dividend determination date" because that's exactly what it is.

The ex-dividend date is the first day of a new dividend quarter and whoever owns the CDx3 Preferred Stock when the stock market opens on the morning of the ex-dividend date gets the dividend for the previous (just ended) quarter.

Therefore, as the ex-dividend date gets closer, the buyers of a share of CDx3 Preferred Stock will tend to bid up the market price offered to you; your shares take on more value as the end of the dividend quarter approaches.

The fact that, given the choice, people would rather have $100 today than the same $100 paid to them three months from now is called the "time value of money." [1]

The time value of money is what drives the Rule of Buyer/Seller Behavior. Investors would rather receive a dividend payment sooner rather than one that occurs later.

---

[1] See Appendix B: CDx3 Special Report *"Calculating Your Rate Of Return"* for a step-by-step walkthrough of the time value of money calculation.

CDx3 Preferred Stocks that are closer to their respective paydays have more value than those that are further away and the market price is pressured upward accordingly.

So now you understand that the market price of a CDx3 Preferred Stock will tend to rise as the end of the dividend quarter approaches (again, this is the general case; we will discuss adjusting for market conditions later).

Back to my original question to you: if I name a CDx3 Preferred Stock, could you tell me what the market price is most likely to be three months from now? The U.S. Securities and Exchange Commission (SEC) gives it away:

"With a significant dividend, the price of a stock may move up by the dollar amount of the dividend as the ex-dividend date approaches…"[2]

> ### #1: Rule of Buyer/Seller Behavior:
>
> Within the short-term period of a dividend quarter and without outside influences, the market price of a CDx3 Preferred Stock will tend to rise as the end of the dividend quarter approaches and do so by the amount of the quarterly dividend.

Remember the objectives of the CDx3 Income Engine - maximize revenue while minimizing risk and work. Because of the Rule of Buyer/Seller Behavior, if you are considering selling a CDx3 Preferred Stock you only need to check the market price one day per quarter – the last day of the dividend quarter when the market price tends to be relatively high, favoring sellers (minimizing work).

---

[2] Source: *www.SEC.gov/answers/dividen.htm* (the missing 'd' is not a typo)

Early Dividend Quarter Price Drop

Just as the upward pressure on the market price of a CDx3 Preferred Stock is highest on the last day of a dividend quarter, price pressure is lowest during the early days of a dividend quarter, just after the ex-dividend date has passed and for all of the same reasons.

Returning to our previous scenario, let's say that I decline your counter offer of $25.49. So the next day, the day of the ex-dividend date, you still own your share of this CDx3 Preferred Stock so you get the $0.50 dividend.

Now that you've collected, you call me back and say "hey Doug, how would you like to buy this CDx3 Preferred Stock share from me today – same price, $25.49?"

Nice try. You already collected the dividend for the quarter. If I buy it from you now, I have to wait another three months to get the next dividend. If you're going to sell a share of CDx3 Preferred Stock in the early days of a dividend quarter (on or shortly after the ex-dividend date), you are going to have to lower your price by about the amount of the quarterly dividend.

For those looking to buy, however, this is an equally great time to look for bargains (much more on this in Part III).

Result: The Quarterly Saw Tooth

Let's look at an example of the Rule of Buyer/Seller Behavior in action. The below chart shows the daily closing market price of another Public Storage CDx3 Preferred Stock, PSA-T, over two full quarters.

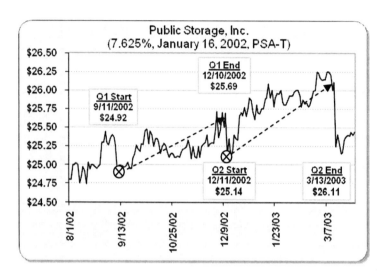

Notice how the Rule of Buyer/Seller Behavior pushes the market price of PSA-T up as the end of the dividend quarter approaches.

Once the ex-dividend date arrives to start the next dividend quarter, the price drops again by approximately the amount of the quarterly dividend (if there are no "outside influences" making it do otherwise – discussed later) and the cycle, predictably, starts over for another quarter.

The resulting saw tooth pattern is visible in the above PSA-T example.

So, back to my question: to determine what the market price of a CDx3 Preferred Stock is most likely to be three months from now you need to look up (1) the most recent ex-dividend date which you can find using your online broker's system or at MarketWatch.com, (2) the closing market price on that day and (3) the quarterly dividend amount that the CDx3 Preferred Stock in question pays.

Add the quarterly dividend amount to the closing market price on the last ex-dividend date. The resulting price is the market price that this CDx3 Preferred Stock is most likely to reach by the end of the dividend quarter three months from now.

In the above PSA-T example, the market price on the first day of the first quarter shown (the ex-dividend date) was $24.92.

PSA-T has a declared dividend rate of 7.625%. That's $1.91 ($25 x 7.625%) per year for every share that you own. Divide $1.91 by four and you get $0.48 as the quarterly dividend paid to you by PSA-T.

Now add that $0.48 to the quarter start price of $24.92. In a perfect market, the most likely market price for PSA-T at the end of the dividend quarter three months later would be $25.40 ($24.92 + $0.48).

The actual price of PSA-T at the end of that first dividend quarter was $25.69, $0.29 more than what we would have expected in a perfect market.

The Rule of Buyer/Seller Behavior pushed the market price right through the roof. What happened?

Characteristics Of An Imperfect Market

The Rule of Buyer/Seller Behavior says that, over a quarter, the market price of a CDx3 Preferred Stock will tend to go up by the amount of the quarterly dividend ($0.48) if there are not any "outside influences" (meaning other market pressures that push the price up or down by more than the amount of the quarterly dividend).

But markets are rarely perfect. Sometimes there will be excess demand that pushes the market price up more than we would expect or, conversely, less market demand resulting in a lower market price.

Continuing with our PSA-T example from the above chart, take a look at the following table:

Qtr Starts On Ex-Dividend Date	Qtr Ends On Day Prior To Next Ex-Dividend Date	Market Price On Quarter Start Date	Market Price On Quarter End Date	Quarterly Price Change
Sep 11, 2002	Dec 10, 2002	$ 24.92	$ 25.69	$ 0.77
Dec 11, 2002	Mar 13, 2003	$ 25.14	$ 26.11	$ 0.97

As shown a moment ago, the market price of PSA-T at the end of the first quarter on December 10, 2002 was not $25.40 as we would expect, but had risen to $25.69 – a full $0.77 increase over the quarter.

Is there "outside influence" beyond the Rule of Buyer/Seller Behavior pushing the market price of PSA-T up? You bet, and a lot of it.

Instead of rising the $0.48 that the Rule of Buyer/Seller Behavior explains, the market price of PSA-T rose $0.77. This indicates that, as of December 10, 2002, there is significant demand in the marketplace for this CDx3 Preferred Stock.

And, looking at the second quarter, that demand continued to grow even further producing a $0.97 price increase.

Because this was happening during a period of decreasing dividend rates, the fact that this older CDx3 Preferred Stock was returning a dividend of 7.625%, compared with the average of about 6.75% being offered by new CDx3 Preferred Stocks at the time, buyers were willing to pay an extra $0.49 to get their hands on your older, higher dividend paying CDx3 Preferred Stock.

> Because of the Rule of Buyer/Seller Behavior, the market price of a CDx3 Preferred Stock will tend to be at or near its peak value for the quarter on the last day of the quarter – the *day prior to* the next ex-dividend date.

The extent to which the Rule of Buyer/Seller Behavior manifests itself will vary, but the upward pressure that it puts on the market price of a CDx3 Preferred Stock, throughout a given dividend quarter, is always present.

Rule #2: The Rule Of Rate/Price Opposition

$25.00 per share is a magical value in the marketplace for CDx3 Preferred Stocks. A new CDx3 Preferred Stock starts its life on its IPO date at this price and, five years later, reaches its call date when the issuing company can call the issue and purchase your shares back from you at $25.00 per share (chapter 14 will show you how to determine the likelihood of a call). Until or unless the issuing company calls the issue, you will continue to receive your quarterly dividends.

What happens to the market price in between the IPO date and the day it is called is driven by the second of our Three Rules of Market Price Predictability – the Rule of Rate/Price Opposition.

While the Rule of Buyer/Seller Behavior affects the market price of a CDx3 Preferred Stock during the short-term period of a dividend quarter, the Rule of Rate/Price Opposition acts upon the market price of a CDx3 Preferred Stock, to one extent or another as we will see, for its entire five year life span and beyond (as long as conditions do not favor a call).

Like the last section, let me start this section with a question: if I name a CDx3 Preferred Stock that has been around for, say, a year or two, can you tell me if its current market price is more likely to be higher or lower than $25 per share (without looking)?

Here's how the Rule of Rate/Price Opposition allows you to answer that question.

Rates Down, Prices Up And Vice Versa

The Rule of Rate/Price Opposition describes the relationship between the declared dividend rate at which companies can issue new CDx3 Preferred Stocks (i.e. the "going dividend rate") and the market price of older, previously issued CDx3 Preferred Stocks.

In short, the direction of the going dividend rate and the market prices of older issues will move in opposite directions; they oppose each other. Rates down, prices up and vice versa.

Look at it this way- let's say that you purchase a new CDx3 Preferred Stock that pays an 8.0% annual dividend. By definition, all newly issued CDx3 Preferred Stocks cost $25 per share so let's further say that this is the price you paid.

After some time goes by you check again and find that new CDx3 Preferred Stocks are now being introduced with a dividend rate of 7.0% (at, as required, a market price of $25); dividend rates are decreasing.

Well, if the current going dividend rate of 7.0% is commanding $25 per share from the buyers of the world, what do you think has happened to the market price of the CDx3 Preferred that you purchased earlier that pays 8.0%? It will tend to exceed $25, of course.

If a 7% CDx3 Preferred Stocks has a market price of $25 then the market price of a previously issued CDx3 Preferred Stock that pays 8%

will tend to be greater than $25. Should you choose to sell, you are looking at a nice capital gain in addition to your 8% dividend income.

Capital gain plus dividend income in the meantime – the CDx3 Income Engine.

In this simple example you can see why, during a period of *decreasing* dividend rates, the market prices of CDx3 Preferred Stocks will *increase*, and vice versa – the Rule of Rate/Price Opposition.

The CDx3 Key Rate Chart

It is the Rule of Rate/Price Opposition that drives the direction of the market prices of CDx3 Preferred Stocks, creating a "buyer's market" or "seller's market" as the going dividend rate goes up and down, respectively.

During the Global Credit Crisis (2007 – 2009) the market prices of CDx3 Preferred Stocks behaved exactly the way that the Three Rules Of Market Price Predictability said they would. That crisis was so extreme that I have devoted an entire chapter to it later in the book.

For now, however, I will use the pre-crisis period of January 2001 through December 2006 to teach you the fundamentals and we'll look at some post-crisis data too. We'll get to the Global Credit Crisis later.

The six year period beginning January 2001 makes a great period for examination because it included periods of both increasing rates and decreasing rates, and in historically long, sustained fashion. This unique period allows us to see the Rule of Rate/Price Opposition in action very clearly.

As you're about to see, when the cost of money is *increasing*, putting upward pressure on CDx3 dividend rates, market prices will tend to decrease. Think about that – high dividend payers available at falling prices – time to consider buying.

But equally true is that the market price that you can command for your CDx3 Preferred Stocks will keep going up and up as long as the "going dividend rate" being offered on newly issued CDx3 Preferred Stocks is *decreasing* – time to consider selling.

In this way, the CDx3 Income Engine continually swings back and forth between favoring dividend income (when dividend rates are going up and we're buying for low prices) and capital gain income (when prices are going back up and we're selling).

Since market prices are obviously sensitive to dividend and interest rates in the U.S. economy, we need an easy way to monitor those rates.

There are a wide variety of rates that are readily available for free that allow us to keep an eye on the "cost of money." For the purposes of preferred stock investing I watch three key rates:

1) The federal funds rate[3] - this is the interest rate that banks charge to borrow money from each other. This rate, and the rest of monetary policy in the U.S., is managed by the U.S. Federal Reserve (the "Fed"). The federal funds rate reflects the cost of money at a very low level in the U.S. economy;

2) The five-year Treasury note ("T-note") yield[4] - this rate reflects the cost of money a bit higher within the U.S. economy. The five-year T-note is available to the investing public and is therefore more volatile than the federal funds rate. I use the five-year T-note since a CDx3 Preferred Stock has a five year call date (CDx3 Selection Criteria number 2). Because the T-note is more volatile, I chart it using a statistical technique called a "three-month moving average"

---

[3] Available at www.federalreserve.gov/datadownload. See Selected Interest Rates.
[4] Also available at www.federalreserve.gov/datadownload. Referred to as "constant maturities/Nominal."

that smoothes out extreme highs and lows so that we can better see what is really going on; and

3) The CDx3 Preferred Stock dividend rate[5]- this is the average declared dividend rate of newly issued CDx3 Preferred Stocks for a given month. The same three-month moving average is used to chart this rate in order to moderate exceptional values so that we can better see trends.

By watching these three key rates CDx3 Investors can actually watch what the "cost of money" is doing at three levels throughout the U.S. economy. The chart that shows us these three key rates is referred to as the "CDx3 Key Rate Chart." Here is the CDx3 Key Rate Chart for the period January 2001 through December 2006 (chapter 4 presents this chart for the Global Credit Crisis period, 2007 through 2009).

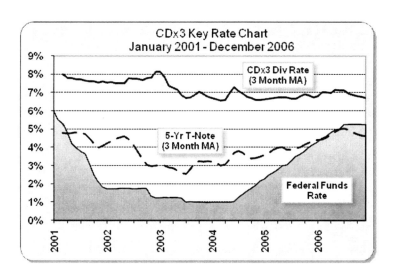

---

[5] Chapter 7 will discuss how to identify newly issued CDx3 Preferred Stocks and their declared dividend rates.

As you can see by looking at the above CDx3 Key Rate Chart, in general the three rates track together. Since all three of these key rates represent a cost of money at one level or another within the U.S. economy over the same period of time, this general consistency is not surprising.

But zooming in, you can see five CDx3 dividend rate changes:

- 2001 to early-2002: decreasing
- Early-2002 to late-2002: increasing
- Late-2002 to mid-2003: decreasing
- Mid-2003 to mid-2006: generally stable, slightly increasing;
- After mid-2006: decreasing.

With the exception of a fairly short-lived period during 2002, CDx3 dividend rates were decreasing between 2001 and mid-2003 when they then bottomed out, decreasing from about 8% to about 6.75%.

We would therefore expect the market price of CDx3 Preferred Stocks to have generally increased between 2001 and mid-2003 with a break in the action during a few months in 2002.

Now that we know what dividend rates were doing during our pre-crisis study period (2001-2006), let's look at a real CDx3 Preferred Stock to see how market prices reacted during the same period.

Meet Empire District Electric Company.

 The Empire District Electric Company (NYSE: EDE) is a public utility located in Joplin, Missouri engaged in the generation, purchase, transmission and distribution of electricity to about 150,000 customers throughout a four state region. On February 23, 2001 EDE introduced its Series D CDx3 Preferred Stock for public sale with a dividend rate of 8.5% (EDE-D).

The following chart shows EDE-D's daily closing market price over the five years between its introduction in early-2001 and its call date in March 2006.

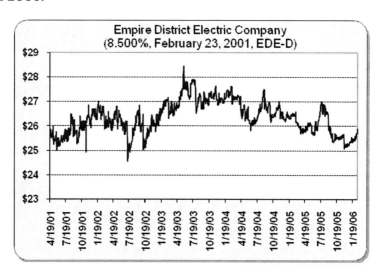

Notice that beginning in early-2001 through early-2002, when CDx3 dividend rates were *decreasing*, the market price of EDE-D was *increasing*. You can also see the market price of EDE-D *decrease* when CDx3 dividend rates *increased* from early-2002 through late-2002.

The Rule of Rate/Price Opposition in action.

#2: Rule of Rate/Price Opposition:

The direction of dividend rates works in opposition to the direction of the market price of CDx3 Preferred Stocks. When the average dividend being offered by newly issued CDx3 Preferred Stocks is decreasing, the market price of older, previously issued CDx3 Preferred Stocks will tend to increase; but when dividend rates go back up, the market price of previously issued CDx3 Preferred Stocks tends to go back down.

The further and faster dividend rates go up or down, the further and faster market prices will go down or up, respectively. We will see a stunning example of this in chapter 4 when we take a look at the marketplace for CDx3 Preferred Stocks during the Global Credit Crisis.

Now take another look at the above chart for EDE-D; specifically, the market price behavior after mid-2003 through early-2006 as EDE-D approached its March 2006 call date. During this period, CDx3 dividend rates were generally stable but slightly increasing. But the market price for EDE-D during this period dropped from about $28 per share down to about $25 per share.

If CDx3 dividend rates were generally stable but slightly increasing during this period, the Rule of Rate/Price Opposition would have us believe that the market price of EDE-D should be stable but slightly decreasing. A drop of $3 per share is not a slight decrease. Has the Rule of Rate/Price Opposition come off its tracks?

No. This is where the last of our Three Rules of Market Price Predictability comes in - the Rule of Call Date Gravity. This rule not only pushes the market price of a CDx3 Preferred Stock in a very predictable manner at a specific point in time and under specific conditions, but does so to a specific dollar amount – one that we will know way in advance.

Rule #3: The Rule Of Call Date Gravity

The Rule of Call Date Gravity is a rule that delivers a great selling opportunity to CDx3 Investors. Therefore, some of this discussion I am going to leave until Part IV when we talk about selling a CDx3 Preferred Stock for a capital gain.

For now, let's understand what the call date is and how it works.

As I did with the previous two rules, let me start the explanation of the Rule of Call Date Gravity with a question: if I were to identify a newly issued CDx3 Preferred Stock, what will the market price be five years from now (assuming no unusual market conditions and within a small margin of error)? Once you understand the Rule of Call Date Gravity you will be able to answer that question (no clairvoyance required).

After explaining how this works, I'll show you a chart of a CDx3 Preferred Stock from Energy East Corporation that illustrates the Rule of Call Date Gravity in action.

When a company issues a preferred stock, they do so at a promised dividend rate that will be paid to you. The issuing company also promises, in the prospectus, to pay you this dividend, each quarter, for a certain minimum period of time; that is, if dividend rates drop, the company cannot cancel your dividend the next day in order to reissue the preferred stock at the new, lower rate.

Once they issue the preferred stock at a declared dividend rate, they're stuck with it – until the call date.

If the issuing company "calls" your shares, the CDx3 Preferred Stock is said to have been "called" or "retired" or "redeemed."

And if the issuing company decides to do so, they must pay you $25.00 per share. It does not matter what the current market price is on the call date nor does it matter what you originally paid for your shares. $25.00 per share, that's what you're going to get.

But the issuing company is not *required* to call (buy back from you) your shares. They will only do so if market conditions favor a call. If market conditions do not favor calls, you will notice that the list of great CDx3 Preferred Stocks available to buyers to pick from just keeps getting longer (2010 – 2011). But don't worry about that now; in chapter 14 I'll show you how to determine if the issuing company is likely to call your CDx3 Preferred Stock or not.

Remember, the call date for every CDx3 Preferred Stock is public knowledge as published in the prospectus. Everyone in the world knows when the call date is and that, if the issue is called, the issuing company is going to pay the holder $25 per share.

So, what do you think happens to the market price of a CDx3 Preferred Stock as the call date approaches (five years after its introduction)? If The Market believes that conditions favor a call, the market price will trend toward $25, of course.

No one is going to pay you much more than that once the issuing company regains the right to purchase the shares back at that price.

Back to my original question: what will the market price of a newly issued CDx3 Preferred Stock be five years from now (assuming no unusual market conditions and within a small margin of error)?

Answer: $25 per share (your friends will be surprised and justifiably impressed). Market conditions have to favor a call, as we will see in chapter 14; but, assuming that they do, there is a 91% chance that the issuing company (your "built-in buyer") will call your shares.

#3: Rule of Call Date Gravity:

If market conditions favor a call, the market price of a CDx3 Preferred Stock will tend to move toward $25.00 per share as the call date approaches.

Let's take a look at the market price behavior of a real CDx3 Preferred Stock that found itself in this very situation as its call date approached in July 2006.

 Energy East Corporation (acquired by Spain-based Iberdrola in 2008 for $4.5 billion) owns several gas and electric utilities serving customers throughout the eastern United States.

On July 18, 2001 Energy East introduced a CDx3 Preferred Stock paying an annual dividend of 8.25% under the trading symbol ECT.

Energy East is obligated to pay holders of ECT this 8.25% annual dividend until ECT's call date on July 24, 2006. On, or at any time after, that date Energy East regains the right to purchase ECT back from its holders by paying them $25 per share.

Here is the closing market price for ECT for its last seven dividend quarters.

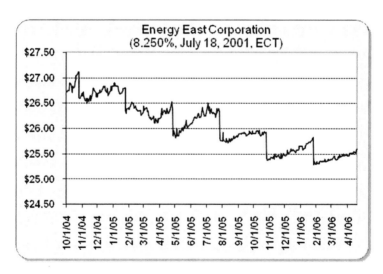

Earlier we saw how the Rule of Rate/Price Opposition makes dividend rates and market prices of CDx3 Preferred Stocks move in opposite directions.

In late-2004 the going dividend rate being paid by the most recently issued CDx3 Preferred Stocks was generally stable although slightly *increasing* all the way through mid-2006. We would therefore expect the market price of a CDx3 Preferred Stock during that period to be generally stable although slightly *decreasing*.

ECT was trading for about $27 as late as October 2004. Since dividend rates remained relatively flat for almost two more years after that time, we would expect the market price of ECT to remain relatively flat as well.

But as illustrated on the above chart the market price of ECT drops significantly during this period.

Rule Versus Rule

What you are seeing in the above chart for ECT is nothing less than the Rule of Call Date Gravity overwhelming the Rule of Rate/Price Opposition in the marketplace for CDx3 Preferred Stocks.

As ECT's July 2006 call date approached The Market clearly believed that conditions favored the call of ECT by Energy East.

In July 2006 the going dividend rate being offered by newly issued CDx3 Preferred Stocks was about 7% but Energy East was still having to pay out quarterly dividends at the annual rate of 8.25% to ECT shareholders.

In chapter 14 we will see an example where a company (Public Storage, Inc.) issued a new CDx3 Preferred Stock at 6.500% in order to generate the cash they needed to call a five year old CDx3 Preferred Stock that was costing them 7.250% in dividend expense; a very common method of "refinancing" a company's dividend expense obligation down to a lower rate.

If market conditions favor a call, the Rule Of Call Date Gravity will overwhelm the Rule Of Rate/Price Opposition as the call date approaches and the market price of a CDx3 Preferred Stock will approach $25 as its call date approaches.

This is important to you as a CDx3 Investor. Knowing that the Rule of Call Date Gravity may pull the market price of your CDx3 Preferred Stock back to $25, and do so at a specific time, helps you to decide when or if to sell your CDx3 Preferred Stock. I'll show you how to determine if market conditions favor a call later in chapter 14.

From a researcher's perspective, the six years between January 2001 and December 2006 provided an excellent study period.

With long sustained periods where dividend and interest rates throughout the U.S. economy either steadily decreased, steadily increased or remained stable, the data from this period of time regarding the market price performance of CDx3 Preferred Stocks is nearly pure.

Because of this level of data purity, we have been able to isolate and identify the corresponding effect on the market prices of CDx3 Preferred Stocks and define the Three Rules of Market Price Predictability.

As you are about to see, the Three Rules of Market Price Predictability apply to the marketplace for CDx3 Preferred Stocks even under the most extreme of conditions.

Let's take a closer look at the period beginning in June 2007 through March 2009 – the period of the Global Credit Crisis.

THE GLOBAL CREDIT CRISIS

The Global Credit Crisis that began in June 2007 and ended in March 2009 ushered in the worst economic downturn in decades including a nasty recession within the U.S. economy.

For CDx3 Investors, however, it delivered the best opportunity for preferred stock investors in history. As I am about to show you, the market prices of CDx3 Preferred Stocks throughout the Global Credit Crisis behaved exactly how the Three Rules of Market Price Predictability said they would.

The ten CDx3 Selection Criteria (see chapter 7) filtered out the 57 preferred stocks from every failed bank – Lehman Brothers, Fannie Mae, Freddie Mac, New Century, Washington Mutual, Bear Stearns, CIT Group, IndyMac – all of them.

And these same ten criteria let pass the specific 13 preferred stocks from the four banks that would be saved – Countrywide (acquired by Bank of America), Merrill Lynch (also by Bank of America), National City Capital (by PNC Financial) and Wachovia (by Wells Fargo).

Here are the results.

CDx3 Selection Criteria Results, Global Credit Crisis

Financial Institution	Preferred Issues	Meet CDx3?	Bankrupt?
Bear Stearns (May 2008)	1	NO	YES
IndyMac (Aug 2008)	0	N/A	YES
New Century (Aug 2008)	2	NO	YES
Fannie Mae (Sep 2008)	16	NO	YES
Freddie Mac (Sep 2008)	21	NO	YES
Lehman Bros. (Sep 2008)	11	NO	YES
Washington Mutual (Sep 2008)	3	NO	YES
CIT Group (Nov 2008)	3	NO	YES
	57		
Countrywide (by Bank of America)	2	YES	NO
Merrill Lynch (by Bank of America)	3	YES	NO
National City (by PNC Financial)	4	YES	NO
Wachovia (by Wells Fargo)	4	YES	NO
	13		

In 70 out of 70 cases, the CDx3 Selection Criteria got it exactly right month after month. During the Global Credit Crisis CDx3 Investors did not miss so much as a single dividend payment; every CDx3 dividend was paid in full and on time throughout the crisis[1].

---

[1] After the Global Credit Crisis had run its course, the U.S. auto industry nearly failed in late-2009. Citizens Republic Bancorp (CRBC), having survived the Global Credit Crisis, serves the auto industry from its headquarters in Flint, Michigan. On January 28, 2010 CRBC deferred the cumulative dividend on its CDx3 Preferred Stock CTZ-A, becoming the only CDx3-compliant issue that has ever done so.

To see how unique the Global Credit Crisis was we can look at the cost of money throughout the U.S. economy prior to and after June 2007.

Here is the CDx3 Key Rate Chart that we developed in the previous chapter (see page 57) covering the pre-crisis period of 2001 through 2006.

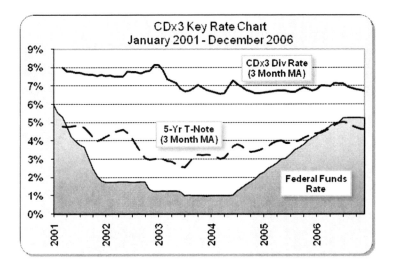

As we saw earlier, while there are some short-lived timing differences, the cost of money at these three levels of the U.S. economy tends to move in fairly consistent fashion. All three key rates generally decreased between 2001 and mid-2003 then headed back up until mid-2006, but at a more gradual pace.

It was the decrease between 2001 and mid-2003 that fed the real estate boom of the same period. As these historically low rates pushed mortgage rates way down, borrowers who could not previously qualify for a home loan suddenly could.

Too many, however, used adjustable mortgages that were only workable as long as rates stayed low. The above chart illustrates the beginning of the end for these borrowers and all things connected to their mortgages as rates headed back up in mid-2004.

Higher mortgage rates followed, taking buyers out of the market which plunged home values just as those earlier adjustable loans started adjusting upward.

Many of these borrowers defaulted on their home loans since they could (a) no longer make the higher payments and (b) were not able to sell their house since the market value of it had dropped below the outstanding balance on their mortgage (their mortgages were "underwater").

Now look at the same three key rates from January 2007 through December 2009.

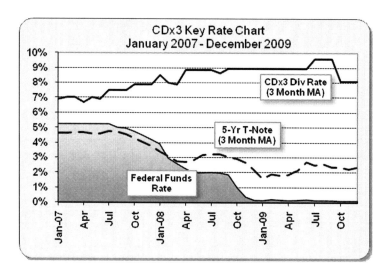

While the federal funds rate (bottom line) and the five-year Treasury note (dotted line) continue to track in fairly consistent fashion, beginning in June 2007 the average dividend rate offered by new CDx3 Preferred Stocks (the "going dividend rate") separated from the other two.

Where the cost of money throughout the U.S. economy has historically shown enormous consistency, that ceased to be the case between June 2007 and March 2009 since it was the banks themselves that were the subject of the crisis.

As home values fell, a variety of investment instruments tied to those home values lost value as well. And as the adjustable mortgage loans from earlier years adjusted upward in 2006 and 2007, borrowers started defaulting on their loans at an astonishing rate.

When loan default rates increase, banks are required to reserve an increasing amount of their cash. Cash-starved banks began increasing the dividend paid by new CDx3 Preferred Stocks, culminating at 9.6% with BBT-B in July 2009, in order to attract investor cash.

These two charts – the first showing the high degree of consistency with the cost of money throughout the U.S. economy prior to the Global Credit Crisis and the second showing the sudden lack of consistency after the Global Credit Crisis got rolling in June 2007 – illustrate just how extreme the economic conditions became during the crisis.

Wall Street Meets Main Street

Throughout the Global Credit Crisis investors became increasingly nervous. The perceived investment risk associated with banks and all other businesses that depend on credit (which is just about all other businesses), increased right along with these fears.

This uncertainty triggered widespread selloffs of U.S. stocks (common and preferreds). Stock investors headed for safer alternatives driving up the price of gold and treasuries (resulting in the dropping yield shown on the above chart for the five year Treasury note).

Foreign investors, including foreign banks, who owned large positions in various investment instruments linked to U.S. mortgages started to see those positions lose value. Foreign banks started having all of the same troubles seen in the U.S. and the world's central banks started dumping massive volumes of cash into the global financial system, along with other measures, in an effort to save them.

U.S. investors started squirreling away tons of cash in savings accounts rather than spend their income. The annualized personal savings rate in the U.S. jumped from 0.6% of disposable personal income at the end of 2007 to 6.9% by the end of May 2009, the highest since December 1993.[2]

Consumer purchases, especially large consumer purchases such as autos and appliances, slowed. This was more bad news for banks. Banks, especially local banks, make money by loaning out the cash that you deposit in savings accounts and CDs at a higher interest rate to borrowers than they are paying you on your savings or CD account.

With savings accounts bulging and far fewer auto and appliances loans being made, banks cut the interest rate offered on CDs from 5.3% in May 2007 (just before the Global Credit Crisis set in) down to 2.9% by March 2009.[3]

As consumption of goods and services fell, layoffs followed. On Monday, December 1, 2008 the National Bureau of Economic Research officially declared that the U.S. economy had slipped into a recession.

---

[2] Bureau of Economic Analysis, U.S. Department of Commerce
[3] 24-month, $10,000 CD; average of top ten U.S. CD yields. Source: *BankRate.com*

Rules Are Rules

The Global Credit Crisis, and the perceived investment risk that came with it, caused the dividend rate being offered by newly issued CDx3 Preferred Stocks to increase from June 2007 through September 2008 when they stabilized at 8.95%.

There was also a big run up in CDx3 dividend rates during 2002 due to uncertainty related to going to war with Iraq.

In both cases, market prices of previously issued CDx3 Preferred Stocks decreased just as the Rule of Rate/Price Opposition says they should – dividend rates up, market prices down.

The Three Rules of Market Price Predictability in general, and the Rule of Rate/Price Opposition in particular, act upon the market price of CDx3 Preferred Stocks as described in chapter 3 *regardless of the reasons why.*

This distinction is very important to you as a CDx3 Investor because it allows you to employ the CDx3 Income Engine without having to concern yourself about the specific issues of the day that are swirling around the U.S. economy.

The Three Rules of Market Price Predictability are independent of the specific reasons that cause investors to buy or sell or for companies to increase or decrease dividend rates. All that matters is that they do so.

What this means for CDx3 Investors is that we are relieved of having to understand the mechanics of the U.S. economy from one day to the next or from having to get a PhD in economics in order to make our investment decisions.

This is a huge benefit to CDx3 Investors. The CDx3 Income Engine provides a structured approach to select, buy and sell the highest quality preferred stocks. And you apply it in consistent fashion during varying economic conditions regardless of the cause of those conditions.

In 2002 it was uncertainly related to war; in 2007 - 2009 it was uncertainty caused by the Global Credit Crisis. What matters for the CDx3 Income Engine in general, and the Rule of Rate/Price Opposition in particular, is that dividend rates were increasing, not the reasons why.

Increased Dividend Yield

Now think about the opportunity that rising CDx3 dividend rates brings to CDx3 Investors. Per the Rule of Rate/Price Opposition, when rates are rising, market prices for CDx3 Preferred Stocks are falling. High dividend payers for dirt cheap market prices – a classic buyer's market.

Remember that since your fixed quarterly dividend is calculated based on $25.00 per share, regardless of your purchase price, your actual annual return ("yield") increases if you can find a way to purchase your CDx3 Preferred Stocks for less than $25 per share (doing so is the subject of Part III).

When the cost of money throughout the economy increases (which many analysts are expecting to be the case during 2012 or 2013), CDx3 Investors use the resulting lower market prices to scoop up dividend-paying shares for low market prices. Always remember that preferred stock investors are paid *based on the number of shares you own*, not the then-current market price or your original purchase price.

The following chart shows the dividend yield provided by the 20 CDx3 Preferred Stocks issued during the Global Credit Crisis (June 2007 through March 2009) when purchased using the method described in Part III.

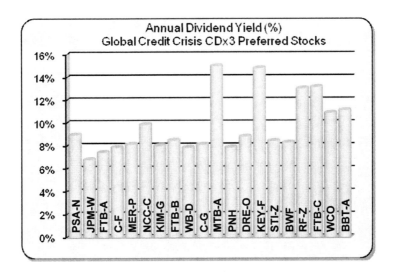

Between June 2007 and March 2009 there were 20 new CDx3 Preferred Stock issued. By knowing when the market price of a CDx3 Preferred Stock tends to favor buyers during a period of increasing rates (as described in Part III), these creations of the Global Credit Crisis provided an average annual dividend yield (before any capital gains) of 9.4% to CDx3 Investors. To see the Effective Annual Return that these 20 CDx3 Preferred Stocks ultimately provided to CDx3 Investors who purchased them at the time, see the results tables on pages 234 and 235.

Whether or not making such purchases would be consistent with your personal financial resources, goals and risk tolerance is a personal decision that only you can make. But when considering the risk reduction provisions of the CDx3 Selection Criteria (discussed in chapter 7), CDx3 Preferred Stocks can provide a very attractive return at acceptable risk for many CDx3 Investors.

Especially during a period of increasing dividend rates as illustrated during the Global Credit Crisis.

The market price of $25 per share is obviously important for CDx3 Investors. You can think of $25 per share as the pivot point on which a teeter-totter moves up and down.

Since CDx3 Investors always purchase their shares for less than $25 per share, knowing when the price is likely to exceed $25 becomes a very nice piece of information to have if you are considering selling for a capital gain.

And since market prices for CDx3 Preferred Stocks move in the opposite direction of the going CDx3 dividend rate, knowing the direction of the market for CDx3 Preferred Stocks becomes important as well.

In the next chapter we'll take a look at how CDx3 Investors can quickly and easily determine the direction of the marketplace for CDx3 Preferred Stocks.

KNOWING MARKET DIRECTION

Throughout the last few chapters I have provided you with a variety of information about the marketplace for preferred stocks, starting out with a description of how preferred stocks are first created and the different types of preferred stocks. The discussion then moved on to focus on why the CDx3 Income Engine is based on preferred stocks rather than bonds, bank CDs or common stocks.

And you now have an understanding of the Three Rules of Market Price Predictability and how they work – regardless of economic conditions.

The CDx3 Income Engine generates both dividend income and capital gain income to provide the effective annual returns that you see itemized in chapter 15 and illustrated on the back cover of this book – annual returns well north of 10%.

While the CDx3 Income Engine *always* produces dividend income for you, it will favor dividend income or capital gain income as economic conditions change over time.

Specifically, when the marketplace for CDx3 Preferred Stocks is in a "buyer's market" you will notice massive drifts of *dividend* income piling up in your brokerage account. Alternatively, when CDx3

Investors are selling during "seller's market" conditions, a greater portion of your income will be coming from *capital gains* (the profit that you earn when you sell a CDx3 Preferred Stock for a market price far greater than your original purchase price).

Before moving onto the mechanics of actually selecting, buying and selling CDx3 Preferred Stocks in the next Part of this book, I want to show you how to determine the type of market for CDx3 Preferred Stocks that prevails at any point in time.

Knowing whether we are in a buyer's market or seller's market is very important and now I'm going to show you how to directly observe the direction and magnitude of the marketplace for CDx3 Preferred Stocks.

Buyer's Market Or Seller's Market

We have already seen how the cost of money within the economy (dividend and/or interest rates) influences the market for CDx3 Preferred Stocks. Fluctuations in the cost of money alter the behavior of the companies that issue CDx3 Preferred Stocks and those who invest in them, creating buying and selling opportunities along the way.

One thing you can say about a period of increasing rates is that it is *always* followed by a period of decreasing rates. Since such cycles rarely last more than a year or two and CDx3 Preferred Stock do not become callable for five years (IPO date to call date), you will generally have more than one opportunity to sell a particular CDx3 Preferred Stock.

Using the five year T-note yield as an indicator of the cost of money throughout the U.S. economy, look at the following chart since January 1980. Do you see any time where an increase was not followed by a decrease within any five year period?

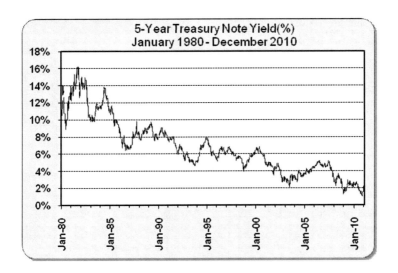

5-Year Treasury Note Yield(%) January 1980 - December 2010

Neither do I. According to the Rule of Rate/Price Opposition, once dividend rates comes back down market prices will tend to head back up, presenting a selling opportunity for you. Until then just keep cashing the quarterly dividend checks.

Buyer's Market

During a "buyer's market" for CDx3 Preferred Stocks, the CDx3 Income Engine favors dividend income generation since CDx3 Investors are buying high dividend paying CDx3 Preferred Stocks at relatively low market prices (well below $25 per share).

As a CDx3 Investor, during a buyer's market you are buying and only buying; selling will come later. Your focus is on adding high dividend paying CDx3 Preferred Stock shares to your CDx3 Portfolio for bargain basement prices (within your personal risk tolerance, of course).

When interest rates are increasing (2012 - 2013?) savvy preferred stock investors are buying, increasing their share count. Doing so not only generates huge amounts of dividend income right now, but creates a great capital gain opportunity for you later once rates come back down and, correspondingly, market prices go back up.

The Global Credit Crisis that began in June 2007 delivered the strongest buyer's market for CDx3 Preferred Stocks in history. CDx3 Investors were able to purchase CDx3 Preferred Stocks with dividend rates close to 9% for about $20 per share, some even lower.

Since your CDx3 Preferred Stock dividend payments are always calculated by multiplying the declared dividend rate by $25.00 (rather than the current market price or the price that you paid when you made your purchase), CDx3 Investors were actually earning much more than the declared dividend rate during the Global Credit Crisis.

For example, purchasing a 9% CDx3 Preferred Stock for $20 per share means that you are actually earning 11.25% per year on the money that you actually have invested ("yield").

During a buyer's market then it is just a matter of knowing when the market price of a CDx3 Preferred Stock is most likely to fall below $25 so that you can be there to take advantage of it. How to do exactly that is described in Part III.

Seller's Market

During a seller's market for CDx3 Preferred Stocks you will be buying and selling so the term "seller's market" is a bit of a misnomer. Part III will show you how to always purchase CDx3 Preferred Stocks for less than $25 per share. For now, let's just focus on how to observe the direction of the marketplace.

A seller's market occurs when dividend rates come back down, pushing the market prices of previously issued CDx3 Preferred Stocks way up above $25 per share (the Rule of Rate/Price Opposition at work here again). CDx3 Preferred Stocks that were purchased for less than $25 per share are suddenly selling for market prices much higher.

How much higher? After increasing during 2002 (due to uncertainly related to war), CDx3 dividend rates came back down the following year, 2003. The CDx3 Preferred Stocks that were purchased by CDx3 Investors during the buyer's market of 2002 were sold during the seller's market of 2003 for an average market price of $27.38 per share.

That's an average capital gain of $2.38 per share on top of the average 7.7% dividend income that CDx3 Preferred Stocks issued during 2002 paid their holders (see page 230 for an itemization of the investment results for each 2002 CDx3 Preferred Stock). $2.38 in capital gain is the equivalent of five quarter's worth of dividend income.

Because CDx3 Investors will start selling some of their CDx3 Preferred Stocks during such conditions, taking advantage of these higher prices, the CDx3 Income Engine favors capital gain income during a seller's market. You'll be learning how to sell for a capital gain in Part IV.

Obviously, it benefits CDx3 Investors to understand whether the market for CDx3 Preferred Stocks is in a "buyer's market" or a "seller's market."

But how can you tell? I am going to show you two methods for directly observing the marketplace for CDx3 Preferred Stocks. The first is provided to subscribers to the CDx3 Notification Service and is called the "CDx3 Perfect Market Index." The second is a "Quick and Easy Index" that you can create yourself without having to subscribe to the CDx3 Notification Service.

The CDx3 Perfect Market Index

There is one thing that all investors crave that they can never have – clairvoyance. Without clairvoyance (or a particularly reliable deck of tarot cards) we are left with examining current and past conditions in order to draw inference regarding the future.

But I think that we can agree that understanding the market conditions we are facing is very meaningful for investors, as imperfect as doing so may be.

This is the CDx3 Perfect Market Index charted through June 2007 just prior to the Global Credit Crisis.

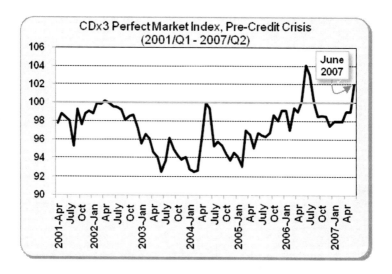

The CDx3 Perfect Market Index uses a proprietary formula that allows us to observe four key aspects of the marketplace for CDx3 Preferred Stocks. Specifically, by looking at the CDx3 Perfect Market Index a CDx3 Investor can quickly see the:

1) type of market we are in, buyer's or seller's;

2) depth of the market we are in;

3) direction of the market indicating whether the buyer's or seller's market is strengthening or weakening; and

4) speed with which it is doing so, gradually or aggressively.

Toward the end of this chapter, I'll describe how you can create an index like this on your own, but for now just focus on the information that the chart provides.

Type Of Market

Since the index is sensitive to changes in the dividend rates and market prices of CDx3 Preferred Stocks, CDx3 Investors can use the index to determine whether CDx3 market conditions favor buyers or sellers.

During a theoretical "perfect market," the market price of a CDx3 Preferred Stock will rise during its dividend quarter (per the Rule of Buyer/Seller Behavior, page 45) by exactly the amount of its quarterly dividend. Then, the following day - the first day of the next dividend quarter – it will fall by exactly the amount of its quarterly dividend.

We saw an example of how an imperfect market produced excess demand for the Series T CDx3 Preferred Stock from Public Storage (PSA-T) on page 50.

By charting how far away today's market conditions (dividend rates and market prices) are from the theoretical perfect market, we can monitor the direction and magnitude of change in the marketplace for CDx3 Preferred Stocks from month to month.

When analyzing the CDx3 Perfect Market Index chart, a value of 100 indicates a theoretical "perfect market." A perfect market is a market that is unencumbered by "outside influences" such as uncertainty related to war (2002), changes in interest rate policy to head off inflation (2006), the onset of a Global Credit Crisis (June 2007) or "quantitative easing" to help a recovery (2010/11).

When the CDx3 Perfect Market Index is below 100 (such as most of the period prior to and following the Global Credit Crisis), the market for CDx3 Preferred Stocks is in a "seller's market."

Similarly, when the CDx3 Perfect Market Index swings above 100, the market for CDx3 Preferred Stock will favor buyers – a "buyer's market."

Looking at the above chart you can see how the CDx3 Perfect Market Index signaled the end of the seller's market and the beginning of the Global Credit Crisis-fueled buyer's market for CDx3 Preferred Stocks in June 2007 when the index jumped above 100.

Depth Of The Market

It's one thing to know whether market conditions favor buyers or favor sellers. But it is also important to know the depth of current market conditions.

By depth I mean "how *close* to a perfect market are we?"

The CDx3 Perfect Market Index shows us not only whether we are in a buyer's market or seller's market, but by seeing how close the current value is to the horizontal line at 100, we can also judge the depth of the current market.

Take a look at how the CDx3 Perfect Market Index measured the depth of the buyer's market for CDx3 Preferred Stocks during the Global Credit Crisis. This is the same chart that you saw a moment ago except I have now extended the timeframe to include the Global Credit Crisis and the recession that followed.

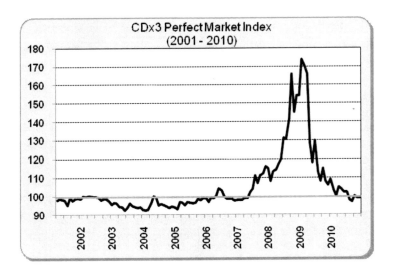

As nasty as it was, the Global Credit Crisis shined a big bright light into some very dark corners of the market for CDx3 Preferred Stocks that are difficult for a researcher to directly observe under more normal conditions.

Notice how the CDx3 Perfect Market Index correctly measured the depth of the buyer's market for CDx3 Preferred Stocks as the credit crisis raged on, month after month.

When you look at the above CDx3 Perfect Market Index chart you are seeing the very face of the Global Credit Crisis as it impacted the market for CDx3 Preferred Stocks. During this period, CDx3 Preferred Stocks, the highest quality preferred stocks available, paying annual dividend rates close to 9% were available for market prices well below $20 per share (that means your actual yield, in many cases, exceeded 11% per year).

Conversely, during a *seller's market* for CDx3 Preferred Stocks (2003, 2010) we would see the CDx3 Perfect Market Index report values well below 100 each month, indicating excess demand for CDx3 Preferred Stock and the higher market prices that result (see the example of excess demand for the Series T CDx3 Preferred Stock from Public Storage on page 52).

Direction Of The Market

Anyone who has been caught inside their car during a flood can tell you that it is not only important to know how deep the water is at the moment but whether or not it is continuing to get even deeper.

The CDx3 Perfect Market Index chart not only tells you how far away from the theoretical perfect market we are (depth), but it also tells us whether or not we are heading toward it or away from it (direction).

The direction of the market for CDx3 Preferred Stocks is determined by simply looking at the slope (up or down) of the CDx3 Perfect Market Index line.

A word of caution here- the CDx3 Perfect Market index chart is not a Ouija board; it cannot tell the future. In terms of indicating direction, it is not "predictive" and should not be used as a forecasting tool.

Having said that, when we were sitting around in June 2008 looking at the prior month's CDx3 Perfect Market Index chart and headlines of bank failures, increasing loan delinquency rates and a confused Federal Reserve Board were in the news every day, it did not take a rocket scientist to guess that the July 2008 index value was likely to head upward, indicating a strengthening of the already historical buyer's market that we were in at the time.

Speed Of The Market

A change in the CDx3 Perfect Market Index of less than five points is within the normal background noise of a normal market. Since market prices for CDx3 Preferred Stocks change all day long there is going to be some movement in the index just as a matter of business being done every day.

A change greater than five points, one way or the other, is considered more significant. And monthly changes in the index beyond ten points will only occur if you've heard about it in the news. By that I mean that changes in the market for CDx3 Preferred Stocks that result in a 10+ point swing in the CDx3 Perfect Market Index only happen as a result of a collection of events that make the financial news for at least a solid week.

One such month was November 2008 when the CDx3 Perfect Market Index dropped from 166 to 145, a whopping decrease of 21 points in one month.

November 2008 was the month when the U.S. Treasury decided to pump hundreds of billions of dollars into cash-starved banks by investing in them. Under its TARP program, Treasury bought 5% custom-made preferred stocks in these banks. Going forward, if the government ever wanted to see their billions again they would have to be certain that these banks did not fail; the government had offered implicit protection to these banks.

The market prices of CDx3 Preferred Stocks offered by these banks shot up by over 35% within weeks, weakening the historic buyer's market for CDx3 Preferred Stocks as illustrated by the CDx3 Perfect Market Index in November 2008. CDx3 market prices returned to their pre-crisis levels in August 2010.

As you'll read later, during a buyer's market, savvy CDx3 Investors know to "keep some powder dry." By looking at the CDx3 Perfect Market Index chart every month during the Global Credit Crisis, it was clear that CDx3 Investors were going to have their pick of the highest quality preferred stocks at rock bottom prices – no tarot cards required.

Later, in chapter 10, I will show you the "CDx3 Bargain Table" that identifies not just the best bargains for you as a CDx3 Investor during such market conditions, but does so in a manner that caters to several common investment objectives.

The CDx3 Perfect Market Index chart is only available to subscribers to the CDx3 Notification Service. However, in the following section I will provide you with a method that you can do on your own, using information that is already available to you, to get a real good idea of the direction of the marketplace for CDx3 Preferred Stocks.

Creating Your Own Quick And Easy Index

Take my word for it – if I were to provide you with a specification of how the CDx3 Perfect Market Index is calculated each month, you would not want to do it on your own. To be statistically valid and comparable from one month to the next to the degree that I, as a researcher, need it to be is substantially more rigorous than most have the patience for.

Fortunately, there is a quick and easy way to get a pretty good sense of what the marketplace for CDx3 Preferred Stocks is doing.

Your objective here is to be able to look at some readily available information in order to assess the market for CDx3 Preferred Stocks. So the first thing you're going to need is a representative list of CDx3 Preferred Stocks to watch – makes sense.

Don't be shy with your list either; the bigger your list the more accurately it will be able to tell you about what's going on in the marketplace for CDx3 Preferred Stocks.

Minimize Bias In Your Index

With this list of CDx3 Preferred Stocks you are creating a sample. The scourge of all people taking samples is that your sample – being just that, a sample rather than the whole population – ends up being biased in one way or another. So we have to do what we can, within reason for our Quick And Easy Index, to minimize the bias in your list.

For example, you do not want to load up your list with multiple CDx3 Preferred Stocks from the same company since a day of good news or bad news about this one company could distort your results substantially. *No more than one* CDx3 Preferred Stock from a given company.

For the same reason you want the CDx3 Preferred Stocks in your list to be issued by companies from *multiple industries.*

Also, you want to use CDx3 Preferred Stocks that are at the *same point within their dividend quarter* to minimize distortion caused by the Rule of Buyer/Seller Behavior (see chapter 3). Since it is very easy to identify CDx3 Preferred Stocks that have just started a new dividend quarter (the ex-dividend date is the first day of a new dividend quarter and this date is readily available online), use CDx3 Preferred Stocks that have just cleared their ex-dividend date for your list.[1]

And try to use CDx3 Preferred Stocks that are *fairly new* so that you do not have to worry about the price distorting effect of the Rule of Call Date Gravity (see chapter 3).

To summarize, for your list you want CDx3 Preferred Stocks that:

1) include no more than one issue from the same company;

2) come from companies representing multiple industries;

---

[1] Most CDx3 Preferred Stocks use the calendar quarter for their dividend quarter. Limiting your list to issues that do so will give you the most choices to pick from.

3) have just cleared their quarterly ex-dividend date; and

4) are fairly new (less than four years old).

With such a list of CDx3 Preferred Stocks in hand, you will be able to use either your online brokerage account or a free website such as Yahoo! Finance (www.finance.yahoo.com) to keep your fingers fairly well placed on the pulse of the CDx3 marketplace.

Let me walk you through setting up a sample Quick And Easy Index that you can create on your own.

Identify Your Candidates

The CDx3 Preferred Stock tables presented in chapter 15 show you the CDx3 Preferred Stocks introduced during each calendar year between 2001 and 2010.

As I am writing this, there are 28 issues that are less than four years old (criteria #4). Of these 28, fifteen cleared their most recent dividend quarter in March 2011 (criteria #3). Of these fifteen there are four issues from duplicate companies (criteria #1), bringing our sample to eleven CDx3 Preferred Stocks.

Symbol	Company	IPO Date	Declared Dividend Rate	Industry
MER-P	Bank of America	Aug 2007	7.375%	National Bank
NCC-C	PNC Financial	Aug 2007	8.000%	Regional Bank
MTB-A	M&T Capital	Jan 2008	8.500%	Regional Bank
DRE-O	Duke Realty	Feb 2008	8.375%	Shopping Ctrs
KEY-F	KeyCorp Capital	Feb 2008	8.000%	Regional Bank
BWF	Wells Fargo	Mar 2008	7.875%	National Bank
BBT-A	BB&T Capital	Sep 2008	8.950%	Regional Bank
JPM-C	JP Morgan	Mar 2010	6.700%	National Bank
KIM-H	Kimco Realty	Aug 2010	6.900%	Office Buildings
PSA-P	Public Storage	Oct 2010	6.500%	Self Storage
PSB-R	PS Business Parks	Oct 2010	6.875%	Office Buildings

This sample is pretty heavy on banks so feel free to trim your results if needed. But I think you get the idea. For our purposes here I'll continue with these eleven.

I have now met criteria #1 (no duplicates), #2 (multiple industries), #3 (just cleared a dividend quarter) and #4 (less than four years old).

We now have eleven candidates for our sample Quick And Easy Index.

Create A Numeric Value

The simplest index that we can use for this list of eleven is the sum of their market prices. By taking note of the current sum value, we can then watch this value change over time in order to gauge changes in the market for CDx3 Preferred Stocks.

Here is our list of eleven CDx3 Preferred Stocks after I set it up as a "watchlist" using TDAmeritrade's online system (you can do this with most online brokerage accounts or Yahoo! Finance in very similar fashion).

Quick And Easy Index						
IVR#: 18	Current market value of list $284.62						
View: Quick And Easy Index	Custom views	Micro Charts		Add Symbol	Add Option Symbols	
Symbol	Description	Ex-Dividend Date	Purchase Price	Last	Gain(%)	Dividend Yield
MER-P	MERRILL LYNCH CAP TR III PFD GTD TR2062	03/10/11	25.32	25.32	0.00	7.2617
NCC-C	NATIONAL CITY CAP TR IV PFD TR ENH2067	03/10/11	26.05	26.05	0.00	7.6628
MTB-A	M&T CAPITAL TRUST IV ENH TRUPS 8.5%	03/10/11	26.69	26.69	0.00	7.9459
DRE-O	DUKE REALTY CORP PFD 1/10 SER O	03/15/11	26.71	26.71	0.00	7.8663
KEY-F	KEYCORP CAP X ENH TRUPS 8.0%	03/10/11	26.09	26.09	0.00	7.6423
BWF	WELLS FARGO CAP XII ENH TRUPS7.875%	03/10/11	26.46	26.46	0.00	7.4546
BBT-A	BB&T CAPITAL TRUST V ENHANCED TR PF	03/10/11	26.98	26.98	0.00	8.2687
JPM-C	JPMORGAN CHASE CAP XXIX GTD CAP SECS	03/29/11	25.50	25.50	0.00	6.5754
KIM-H	KIMCO RLTY CORP PFD CL H	03/30/11	24.88	24.88	0.00	6.9277
PSA-P	PUBLIC STORAGE PFD SHS SER P	03/11/11	25.31	25.31	0.00	6.4052
PSB-B	PS BUSINESS PKS INC CALIF DEP SHS 1/1000	03/14/11	24.63	24.6301	0.00	6.9249

When I set up this watchlist I set my "purchase price" so that it would be the same as the current market price (the "Last" column). While not shown here, I also set the number of shares for each issue to one (more on this in a moment).

Assessing The CDx3 Market With A Quick And Easy Index

You can determine all sorts of things from this list including the direction of market prices for CDx3 Preferred Stocks, what industries are seeing increasing or decreasing demand and whether we are in a buyer's market or seller's market.

You want to be sure to do so (evaluate the market as I am about to show you) in the days that follow the last ex-dividend date from your list.

Continuing with our example, that means in the days following March 30 you want to check the pulse of the marketplace for CDx3 Preferred Stocks. Here's how.

Direction of market prices: First, look at the dollar amount in the grey bar toward the top, $284.62. This is the current "value" of the CDx3 Preferred Stocks that make up my watchlist (this is why I set the Quantity field to a one when I set up the watchlist earlier).

The system automatically calculates this number every time I look at the watchlist by multiplying the current market price (the column labeled "Last" for last trade) by the quantity of shares I said that I owned (one).

This number is the current total value of the CDx3 Preferred Stocks that make up my Quick And Easy Index and the system updates it for me all day every day in real time.

If this number grows month after month you know that market prices for CDx3 Preferred Stocks are rising; if this value is getting lower, it is an indication that overall market prices are falling.

Demand by industry: When I set up the watchlist I also entered the then-current market price as my purchase price. You can see the purchase price values that I entered under the Purchase Price column when the watchlist is displayed.

Notice that the Last column shows the value of the last trade (the current market price) for each CDx3 Preferred Stock. You can see that the marketplace for CDx3 Preferred Stocks was in a seller's market when the above watchlist was created in early 2011; many of the current market prices are above $25 per share.

With the Purchase Price and the Last values available, the system can calculate how much the market price (Last) of each CDx3 Preferred

Stock has gone up or down since you created your watchlist. The result is displayed in the Gain column.

The Gain column is the amount (expressed as a percentage) of change in the market price of each CDx3 Preferred Stock. By becoming familiar with the industries represented in your list of CDx3 Preferred Stocks (see table on page 91), you can quickly see which industries have increasing or decreasing demand in the marketplace.

Buyer's market or seller's market: If the average market price of CDx3 Preferred Stocks falls below $25 the market favors buyers (a buyer's market); conversely, if the average market price is above $25 then the market favors sellers (a seller's market).

The quickest way to monitor the type of market we are in is to look at the average market price of the CDx3 Preferred Stocks that make up your Quick and Easy Index.

To do this, divide the total value ($284.62) by the number of CDx3 Preferred Stocks that make up your list (eleven). In this example, the result is $25.87 ($284.62 divided by 11), indicating that we are in a seller's market for CDx3 Preferred Stocks.

In this Part of *Preferred Stock Investing* you have learned about the marketplace for CDx3 Preferred Stocks. You now have a general understanding of how new CDx3 Preferred Stocks are introduced to the market, the Three Rules of Market Price Predictability that influence the market price at specific times and in specific ways and how to directly observe marketplace behavior over time, be it a buyer's market or a seller's market.

Here's an update to the CDx3 Income Engine Summary Table so that you can more easily keep track of your progress.

CDx3 Income Engine Summary Table

	CDx3 MARKETPLACE DIRECTION	
	Buyer's Market	**Seller's Market**
HOW TO TELL (Part I)	▪ Dividend rates increasing ▪ Market prices < $25 per share ▪ CDx3 Perfect Market Index >100	▪ Dividend rates decreasing ▪ Market prices > $25 per share ▪ CDx3 Perfect Market Index <100
SELECTING (Part II)	▪ CDx3 Selection Criteria ▪ SEC EDGAR system ▪ Watchlist (one for each quarter) ▪ CDx3 Preferred Stock catalog	▪ CDx3 Selection Criteria ▪ SEC EDGAR system ▪ Watchlist (one for each quarter) ▪ CDx3 Preferred Stock catalog

BUYING
(Part III)
	▪ New issues > Over-The-Counter
	▪ CDx3 Bargain Table
	  - < $25 per share
	  - Early in dividend quarter
	  - Old issues > 2nd dividend qtr
	▪ Big Bank TRUPS
	▪ CDx3's Beyond Call Date
		▪ New issues > Over-The-Counter
		▪ CDx3 Bargain Table
		  - < $25 per share
		  - Early in dividend quarter
		▪ Big Bank TRUPS
		▪ CDx3's Beyond Call Date

SELLING (Part IV)	▪ Enjoy dividend checks; do not sell during a buyer's market ▪ Check for "upgrades"	▪ Market price > Target Sell Price; or ▪ Called by issuing company for $25 ▪ Last day of dividend quarter ▪ Check for "upgrades"

Now it's time to put this knowledge to work. In Part II I am going to show you how to select the highest quality preferred stocks.

PART II

Selecting The Highest Quality Preferred Stocks

I REALLY REALLY enjoyed reading your incisive article "Assessing the Risk of CDx3 Preferred Stocks" in the subscriber's newsletter CDx3 Research Notes. What a terrific analysis.

- M.K.Y.

Preferred stock investors want the same thing that every other investor wants – the highest return at the lowest risk.

But, looking at the 1,000 to 2,000 preferred stocks that are available to you at any time, which one do you pick?

The CDx3 Income Engine method of investing in preferred stocks relies on just the highest quality preferred stocks – those that, my research shows, provide respectable returns at acceptable risk. Specifically:

- ✓ Chapter 6 shows you the ten CDx3 Selection Criteria that allow you to identify the highest quality preferred stocks while filtering out the pretenders;

- ✓ Chapter 7 discusses some of the risks that come with investing in preferred stocks and teaches you to use the CDx3 Selection Criteria to help manage those risks; and

- ✓ Chapter 8 quantifies the risks associated with CDx3 Preferred Stocks and identifies issues that The Market may have mispriced, given the investment risk.

THE CDx3 INCOME ENGINE OBJECTIVES

The Global Credit Crisis began in June 2007 and, despite the unprecedented efforts of the world's central banks, continued unabated. Fortunes were lost as the common stocks of many of the world's financial institutions lost almost all of their value. The dividend paid to the holders of these company's common stock was reduced to, in some cases, as low as $0.01 per share (or even eliminated entirely).

Those relying upon common stock dividends for their income, mostly retirees, saw their monthly income shrink accordingly.

Banks started failing – IndyMac, Freddie Mac, Fannie Mae, Bear Stearns, Lehman Brothers, Washington Mutual, New Century, CIT Group – eliminating the dividends from these institutions altogether.

In addition to the common stocks themselves, mutual funds with positions in these financial institutions lost their value as well. Bank executives were getting fired left and right and clients were asking their brokers and financial advisors questions that there were no answers to.

And yet, during all of this mayhem the ten CDx3 Selection Criteria successfully filtered out the preferred stocks from every failed bank, protecting CDx3 Investors from the plight that had stricken millions of others.

As itemized by the table on page 124, the ten CDx3 Selection Criteria (chapter 7) functioned perfectly in 70 out of 70 cases. Even though many common stock dividends saw substantial cuts, the dividends earned from CDx3 Preferred Stocks just kept on coming.

When I started researching the market price behavior of preferred stocks in 2002, I established three specific objectives that I was looking to meet: (1) maximize revenue while (2) minimizing risk and (3) minimizing work.

These three objectives focused my research then and continue to do so today. Every aspect of the CDx3 Income Engine is driven by this simple triangle.

Objective #1: Maximize Revenue

The revenue that one makes from an investment is measured by the effective annual return. The effective annual return can be calculated when you know the purchase price, the sell price, the declared dividend rate and the length of time the investment was held (i.e. how many dividend payments you received).

The CDx3 Income Engine is designed to produce revenue in excess of 10% per year. It does so by piling a downstream capital gain on top of above average dividend income. Since the declared annual dividend rates paid by CDx3 Preferred Stocks range from 6.5% and 9%, getting over the 10% hump is not that tough – if you know when to sell (which is the subject of Part IV of this book).

Here is the effective annual return generated by the CDx3 Income Engine since January 2001 (using all CDx3 Preferred Stocks).

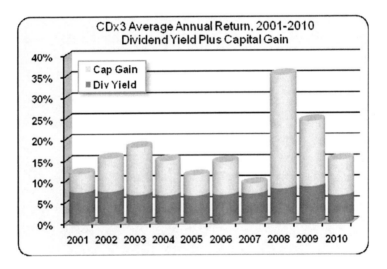

Note that the Global Credit Crisis that began in June 2007 ushered in the largest buyer's market for CDx3 Preferred Stocks in history. Cash strapped banks pushed dividend rates way up throughout 2008 and 2009. Using the Target Sell Price as a guide (see chapter 13), CDx3 Investors were able to sell these high payers for incredible returns throughout 2010 when "seller's market" conditions returned.

To see where my annual averages come from, take a look at chapter 15 where I itemize the effective annual return that you would have earned from each CDx3 Preferred Stock issued since January 2001.

The first objective of the CDx3 Income Engine, maximize revenue, means that we are looking to earn an effective annual return of at least 10% from our CDx3 Preferred Stock investments.

Objective #2: Minimize Risk

What is low risk to one investor may be unacceptably high risk to another so this objective is hard to precisely quantify.

A way of getting around this problem is to use a yardstick that everyone is familiar with and then compare the risks inherent with preferred stock investing to that yardstick.

Since risk is a relative term ("high risk compared to what?"), we need to compare preferred stock investment risk to the risk of an alternative investment that everyone is familiar with.

Certificates of Deposit (CDs) that you buy at your local bank serve this purpose nicely. Those new to investing as well as seasoned day traders and retired brokers all have a common understanding of what a bank CDs is, how it works and, for our purpose here, the level of risk that comes with a bank CD.

Preferred stocks carry more investment risk than bank CDs but the rewards are far greater as well. When I talk about the objective to "minimize risk" what I am looking for is a way to invest in select preferred stocks that, as a group, get the level of investment risk as close to that of a bank CD as I can get it.

Another point regarding the investment risk profile of bank CDs - the federal government learned many valuable lessons from the savings and loan crisis of the late-1980's, one of which was that the $100,000 insurance *per account* was way too generous. Depositors were smart enough to figure out that all they had to do with their $1 million retirement nest egg was spread it over multiple accounts. The claims by depositors when the savings and loan industry melted put the insurer (the Federal Savings and Loan Insurance Corporation – FSLIC) out of business.

The federal government no longer extends their insurance on a per account basis. Rather, since the savings and loan crisis, the current coverage is per *depositor*. Insuring that $1 million retirement nest egg over a number of accounts no longer protects you (you have to use multiple banks, which very few CD depositors take the trouble to do).

The trampoline-sized safety net that we use to enjoy underneath bank CDs is now more like a postage stamp.

But I think that we can agree that compared to other fixed-income investment alternatives, CDs are a low risk choice. My "minimize risk" objective then is to get as close to that level of risk as I can while still meeting the other two CDx3 Income Engine objectives.

Objective #3: Minimize Work

Just so that it's clear, when I say "minimize work" I am talking about doing so without having to subscribe to the CDx3 Notification Service in order to meet this objective. While it is true that subscribers to the CDx3 Notification Service extend minimum work toward managing their CDx3 Portfolio, you can implement the CDx3 Income Engine on your own by following the explanation and resources provided throughout this book.

What good is an investment method if it requires so much work that no one on the planet would have any interest in doing it? Very few people, given the choice, hope to spend endless hours day after day hunched over their computer staring at stock charts.

That's what "day traders" do. In addition to the enormous penalty to their golf game, social life and other obligations, most of them lose money.

And what might be minimum work to one investor may be a completely unacceptable workload for another, so we have the "relative term" problem again just like we did with "minimize risk."

Somewhere between not even needing to get out of bed in the morning and becoming a day trader is an amount of work that most of us would find acceptable when managing our preferred stock portfolio.

Just as we did with the last objective - minimize risk - we have to establish a common understanding of what constitutes an acceptable, but minimum amount of work needed to manage your preferred stock investments. We need another yardstick that is familiar to everyone.

To manage our bank accounts we all spend a certain amount of time each month checking over the bank statements. It does not take much work and there is benefit to knowing that you and your bank are in agreement about what's going on with your money (including how much you think you have).

In other words, we know that most people find that the amount of work needed to review their monthly bank statements is an acceptable amount of work, given the benefits.

The CDx3 Income Engine will allow you to be a successful CDx3 Investor without extending any more work than you already do in order to review your monthly bank statements – that's our yardstick. While you may choose to expend more effort, you will not need to do so in order for the CDx3 Income Engine to work for you.

So now you know the three objectives of the CDx3 Income Engine and what is meant by each one:

1) Maximize Revenue: 10%+;

2) Minimize Risk: As close to a bank CD as we can get; and

3) Minimize Work: No more effort than looking over your bank statement.

Let's move on to the implementation of these objectives, the business of selecting the highest quality preferred stocks from all of the pretenders.

SEVEN

IDENTIFYING CDx3 PREFERRED STOCKS

Most preferred stock investors do not just want a big list of preferred stocks to look at; rather, they want to know how to invest in them.

With the exception of the CDx3 Notification Service, other websites that provide lists of preferred stocks do not (a) identify CDx3 Preferred Stocks nor do they (b) provide any information whatsoever regarding the best time to consider buying or selling preferred stocks.

They simply provide lists of preferred stocks of widely varying accuracy and currency. Anything beyond that is up to you.

There are a variety of resources that allow you to view lists of preferred stocks – some are free while others request a fee. All have their strengths and weaknesses. I have listed them in Appendix A for your reference.

This is largely due to the fact that gathering and filtering such data can be time consuming and therefore costly. When we send out a CDx3 Buyer's Notification message[1] making subscribers aware of a new CDx3

---

[1] Described on page 252.

Preferred Stock, for example, we compile data from six different sources in order to validate our information.

Consequently, those who put in the time and bear the costs for preferred stock lists often request a fee (including the CDx3 Notification Service).

Be forewarned; this is one area where there is a direct relationship between the ease of getting your hands on the information you are after and the cost associated with doing so.

Meet Uncle EDGAR

When a company is going to be issuing a new preferred stock they are required to file a form with the U.S. Securities and Exchange Commission (SEC). The SEC provides a very powerful web-based service that allows you to see recent filings for free called the Electronic Data Gathering and Retrieval system – EDGAR.

EDGAR provides a variety of search capabilities that can be, at times, confusing and mind boggling.

However, the SEC is the official source of all corporate filings and if you want to identify CDx3 Preferred Stocks for free you have to use EDGAR.

You can access EDGAR at:

http://www.sec.gov/edgar/searchedgar/webusers.htm.

Here is what the EDGAR website looks like.

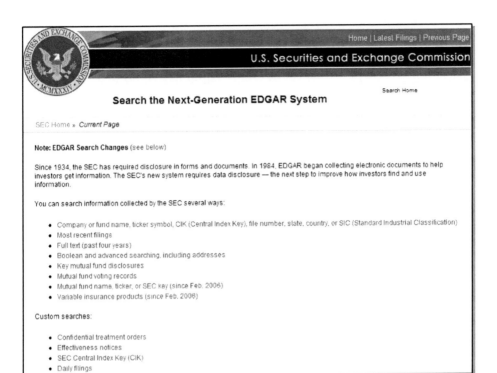

No government agency would be complete without a lot of forms, each of which have several versions and form numbers. The SEC is no exception.

When companies issue a new preferred stock they almost always use SEC form number 424(b)(5), 424(b)(4), 424(b)(2), SWF or FWP. The good news is that EDGAR allows you to search by form number; the bad news is that these same forms are used for many different purposes, not just for issuing new preferred stocks.

From the EDGAR website click on "Most recent filings" and you will be presented with the page that allows you to search by form number.

Remember, this EDGAR page performs a search of the "most recent filings" only so you will need to do this regularly (several times per week). The SEC also provides search tools that allow you to search historical filings as well as the actual text of filings, rather than just searching by form number or company name. If using the Most Recent Filings form type search is too bothersome you might try one of these other options.

Learning to use EDGAR is time consuming and cumbersome; but it is the mother lode of all filings and it is free. If you want to do this for free, you are going to have to get to know EDGAR.

If you would rather someone else do the work for you there are choices other than the CDx3 Notification Service. However, these other sites present entirely unfiltered lists of preferred stocks and provide no information, analysis or strategy regarding the market conditions that tend to favor the buyers and sellers of preferred stocks whatsoever.

For that we offer the CDx3 Notification Service which you can read more about in chapter 18 and at www.PreferredStockInvesting.com.

The CDx3 Selection Criteria

One of my investment philosophies is "stick with the sure thing" rather than taking a chance that something with a higher pay off potential will materialize. This philosophy, as you will come to see, is woven throughout every aspect of the CDx3 Income Engine, including the CDx3 Selection Criteria.

To qualify as a CDx3 Preferred Stock, a regular preferred stock must meet selection criteria that are designed to support the three objectives of the CDx3 Income Engine – maximize revenue while minimizing risk and minimizing work.

The computer models that I use to research the market price behavior of preferred stocks allow for the specification of a filter (selection criteria). Tightening or loosening the filter either lets fewer or more preferred stocks through, respectively.

If the filter is too tight (too many selection criteria), you virtually eliminate your investment risk (the good news) but you've done so by eliminating all preferred stocks from consideration (the bad news); that is, there is nothing left to invest in.

On the other hand, if the filter is too forgiving you wind up with lots of preferred stocks to choose from but the risk associated with doing so goes up as well.

By iteratively adjusting the computer model, I was able to identify ten specific selection criteria – the filter – that produce results that meet our three objectives. The ten winning criteria, as a group, are referred to as the "CDx3 Selection Criteria."

In the following pages I will present the CDx3 Selection Criteria and then a table that shows you how each of these ten criteria support the three objectives of the CDx3 Income Engine discussed in the last chapter.

To be considered a CDx3 Preferred Stock, a regular preferred stock must:

1) Pay a fixed dividend rate of at least 6.5%;

2) Become callable five years after IPO;

3) Pay dividends quarterly;

4) Be rated "investment grade" by Moody's Investors Service;

5) Be issued by a company that has a perfect track record of never having suspended the dividend payments on a preferred stock (and these are mostly decades old, multi-billion dollar companies);

6) Have a "cumulative" dividend obligation;

7) Be issued by a U.S. company;

8) Not be convertible to common stock in the future;

9) Have easy (online) access to the prospectus at IPO; and

10) Have an initial share value (par) of $25.00.

Very important note: notice that these criteria do not select or eliminate preferred stocks from any specific industry; they just select the highest quality issues. If you are after preferred stocks from industries other than those that result from applying these criteria you are going to have to take more risk (i.e. eliminate one or more of these criteria). These criteria result in the highest quality issues *regardless of industry.*

These ten selection criteria allow you to select the highest quality preferred stocks from the 1,000 to 2,000 trading every day. As an investor, having an objectively and consistently applied set of criteria upon which you base your investment decisions is far superior to relying on emotion – either elation or fear.

#1 Pay a fixed dividend rate of at least 6.5%

Regular high quality preferred stocks typically come with declared dividend rates ranging from 6.0% to 9.0%. On the low end, CDx3 Preferred Stocks draw the line at 6.5% (on the high end there is no fixed limit – we'll be happy to take as much as they want to give us).

The reason we are leaving 0.5% of room beneath our floor rate of 6.5% becomes important to our selling strategy which you'll learn about in Part IV. But 0.5% in the world of CDx3 Preferred Stocks is a lot of room; in fact, the CDx3 Perfect Market Index (see chapter 5) can measure changes in the behavior of buyers and sellers of CDx3 Preferred Stocks when the average dividend rate being offered by new CDx3 Preferred Stocks changes as little as 0.25%.

Also avoid "variable dividend rate" issues where the dividend rate varies depending on various, currently unknown, conditions (stick with the sure thing). Whatever the dividend rate being paid on the CDx3 Preferred Stock is, we're going to turn it into much more so there is no reason to take the risks associated with variable rate preferred stocks.

#2 Become Callable Five Years After IPO

The issuing company of a CDx3 Preferred Stock regains the right to purchase your shares back from you, at $25.00 per share, five years after the issue is introduced to the marketplace. This date, five years after the IPO date, is referred to as the "call date" (or "redemption date").

By selecting preferred stocks that become callable five years after their IPO date we are able to switch on the power of the Rule of Call Date Gravity (see page 60).

When the whole world knows that on a specific future date the issuing company of your preferred stock can purchase it from whomever owns it any time they wish, and if they do they are required to pay a specific price per share, the market price can behave very differently as that date approaches.

Knowing what the market price of any investment is likely to be at some future point is a rare gift. By selecting only preferred stocks that have a known, fixed call date we bestow that rare gift onto ourselves.

We want to fix the call date at a specific, known point in time for CDx3 Preferred Stocks. Doing so allows us to take advantage of the known changes in the market price that your CDx3 Preferred Stock may realize as the call date approaches. In chapter 14 I'll show you how to take advantage of an approaching call date.

#3 Pay Dividends Quarterly

This selection criteria provides another point of integration with the Three Rules of Market Price Predictability (chapter 3).

By selecting preferred stocks that all pay their dividends quarterly we can use the Rule of Buyer/Seller Behavior (page 45) to buy and sell CDx3 Preferred Stocks at a point in time that is known in advance.

The Rule of Buyer/Seller Behavior tells us that the market price of a CDx3 Preferred Stock will tend to rise as payday (the ex-dividend date) approaches, assuming no extraordinary "outside influences."

As I will show you in Parts III and IV, because of this rule, CDx3 Investors purchase their CDx3 Preferred Stocks early within the issue's dividend quarter – a time that favors buyers since the market price tends to be relatively low.

Similarly, we tend to sell late in the dividend quarter when market prices tend to be relatively high, favoring sellers (discussed in Part IV).

By fixing the length of the dividend period over which the Rule of Buyer/Seller Behavior plays out for all of your CDx3 Preferred Stocks, you are able to approach your buying and selling decisions with complete consistency. You will always be buying and selling when the market price tends to most favor your doing so, hence maximizing your current dividend yield and downstream capital gain opportunities.

#4 Moody's Investment Grade

As individual investors who are generally not spending their days researching companies and markets, but want to invest in them, we need a way to compare the relative investment risk associated with one alternative to another.

There are three primary companies that rate the long-term credit worthiness of companies and their preferred stocks: Moody's Investors

Service, Standard & Poor's and Fitch Ratings. Mostly for accessibility reasons, Moody's ratings are used for the purpose of helping to identify CDx3 Preferred Stocks.

Moody's Investors Service is a subsidiary of Moody's Corporation which employs about 2,900 employees in 22 countries. Their analysts are experts on specific industries, the companies within those industries and the specific activities of those companies.

Moody's core business is to know these companies and their activities well enough to pass judgment, given a very specific set of standardized criteria, on the company's credit worthiness – good to know when you are considering purchasing a preferred stock.

Moody's puts it this way (I have shortened this for presentation here):

> "Credit ratings and research help investors analyze the credit risks associated with fixed-income securities. Such independent credit ratings and research also contribute to efficiencies in fixed-income markets and other obligations...by providing credible and independent assessments of credit risk."

By specifying that CDx3 Preferred Stocks must be among the highest rated by Moody's (referred to as "investment grade" as opposed to "speculative grade") you, as a CDx3 Investor, automatically realize the benefits of the accumulated knowledge and judgment of the Moody's analysts regarding the issuing company. The label "investment grade" speaks for itself.

The Global Credit Crisis identified some holes in the way credit agencies produce their ratings. One of the major problems was that the massive mortgage foreclosure rate that began in late-2007 exceeded the limits of their statistical models; statistical models that have been honed over many decades and acknowledged worldwide for their uncanny accuracy.

Despite their flaws, the fact is that individual investors have little choice but to rely on these ratings as a proxy for investment risk.

Using an alphanumeric scale, Moody's investment grade rating category includes ten sub-categories: A for really good, B for pretty good, etc. Then they started slicing the boloney really thin – Ba is slightly better than B and Baa is a little bit better than Ba and Baa3 (and higher) is "investment grade." What they ended up with is the following scale, highest to lowest:

Aaa, Aa1, Aa2, Aa3, A1, A2, A3, Baa1, Baa2, Baa3

In the next chapter I'll show you an interesting analysis that compares how closely Moody's and The Market agree regarding the investment risk of CDx3 Preferred Stocks.

Investment grade means what it says, and it is very difficult for a company to obtain and maintain this rating from Moody's. To be considered a CDx3 Preferred Stock, Moody's has to provide it with an investment grade credit rate – Baa3 or higher.

You can use Moody's website (www.Moodys.com) to look up the current rating of a CDx3 Preferred Stock. The easiest way is to use the CUSIP[2] number. You must register with Moody's first but there is no fee requested.

If you want to read more about Moody's credit worthiness rating system, you can go to the State of California Treasurer's website at www.treasurer.ca.gov/ratings/moodys.asp (among many other sites).

---

[2] CUSIP stands for Committee on Uniform Security Identification Procedures and is a standard security identification numbering system. Every CDx3 Preferred Stock has a unique CUSIP number.

www.PreferredStockInvesting.com

#5 No Suspended Dividends - Ever

In order to be considered a CDx3 Preferred Stock a regular preferred stock must meet all ten CDx3 Selection Criteria. By looking over the resulting survivors they really jump out at you. These are multi-billion dollar outfits, most with recognizable names, some not.

For the most part, what you end up with are America's top companies. Companies that, in most cases, are several decades old and many have been in business for well over 100 years.

But for one of their preferred stocks to qualify as a CDx3 Preferred Stock they have to have a perfect track record of never having suspended dividends on a preferred stock – ever.[3]

Unless you are a subscriber to the CDx3 Notification Service (in which case this research is done for you), figuring out if a company has a perfect track record with their preferred stock dividends can be a bit time consuming (not to mention tedious).

For a particular preferred stock that you may be considering, the quickest way to see if the issuing company has ever suspended its dividends is to contact the company's Investor Relations department (see the company's website) and ask them.

Remember, as a publicly traded company it would be very unlikely (and incredibly irresponsible) for them to provide you with misinformation in answer to this question. They are required by law to disclose this information under federal penalty. You may have to ask more than one person as a newbie who answers the phone may not know the answer.

There is also a great online resource. Using a web page at MarketWatch.com you can look up the dividend track record of any preferred stock that you may be considering.

---

[3] My data on preferred stock suspensions goes back to 1936.

I'll use an example to show you how to view the dividend history (or lack thereof) of a preferred stock using MarketWatch. But before I launch into my example, allow me to ask a question: would it make sense to borrow $100 and then pay your lender, say, $100,000 in interest?

On March 24, 1936 Consolidated Edison introduced a new preferred stock with the trading symbol ED-A, and they have been paying out a 5% dividend to its shareholders every quarter since then.

Here's how to use MarketWatch.com to see the dividend payment history (or lack thereof) of a preferred stock. First, point your web browser to www.MarketWatch.com. In the upper right corner you will see a trading symbol search field.

Remember from page 40 that different online services have adopted different trading symbol conventions for preferred stocks. MarketWatch uses the "PR" convention where the hyphen in the trading symbol is replaced by the letters "PR" so ED-A is EDPRA at MarketWatch. Type EDPRA in the trading symbol search field and click the search button.

The current market activity surrounding the granddaddy of all preferred stocks is displayed, including its current market price and a nifty little chart that shows today's trading (usually very low volume for ED-A).

A quick way to access the dividend history is to now click on the Charts tab located just below the security name (and just above the current market price). Doing so takes you to the web page that we are after. You will see another chart with a bunch of chart options on the left side. Drop down the Time to be charted, click on "All data" then Draw Chart.

Your screen will refresh with the chart now showing the entire trading history including the entire dividend payment history for your preferred stock marked with the letter D in a box. A missing D indicates a missed dividend.

For ED-A, this is quite a chart. When you use this technique with preferred stocks that you are considering the chart will not be nearly as cluttered.

#6 "Cumulative" Dividend Obligation

In addition to meeting all of the other CDx3 Selection Criteria, to be considered a CDx3 Preferred Stock, a regular preferred stock must carry the "cumulative" dividend obligation.

More than any other single CDx3 Selection Criteria, it is this cumulative requirement that saved CDx3 Investors from failed banks during the Global Credit Crisis. Once you understand what it means, I think you'll see why.

At the beginning of this chapter I showed you how to locate the prospectus of a preferred stock for free (the SEC's EDGAR system). The prospectus of a preferred stock is a legal document that the issuing company must file with the SEC and explains the obligations and limitations placed on the issuing company with respect to the particular preferred stock issue.

The prospectus will include language that defines whether or not the issuing company is allowed to defer (delay until a future time) or suspend (cancel outright) your dividends.

In cases where the issuing company may defer, but not suspend, your dividend payment(s) the preferred stock is said to be "cumulative." So in the unlikely event that the issuing company runs into a cash crunch and is unable to pay your dividend on time, their obligation to ultimately pay you that dividend does not go away; it accumulates. They still owe you the money.

Has it ever happened? Yes. Once. See the footnote on page 68.

In most cases where the preferred stock is cumulative, words to that effect will be pretty hard to miss when viewing the prospectus and are often located right in the title on the first page. Other times the key language will be a bit harder to find but using your web browser's search function while viewing the prospectus can be a big help.[4]

Here's an example from the prospectus of a 2011 CDx3 Preferred Stock from Public Storage (PSA-Q, 6.500%, April 7, 2011):

> "Distributions on the Preferred Shares **will be cumulative** from the date of issue and will be payable quarterly on or before March 31, June 30, September 30 and December 31, commencing June 30, 2011..."

The prospectus of a cumulative preferred stock will then go on to describe the conditions under which the issuing company is allowed to defer a dividend and when they are obligated to pay you back (usually with interest).

While we can be sympathetic, understanding and show a little patience during extreme circumstances (terrorism, natural disasters), the CDx3 Selection Criteria do not allow the issuer of CDx3 Preferred Stocks to simply walk away from the obligation they have to CDx3 Investors. They must ultimately pay you any deferred dividends.

And remember, issuers of CDx3 Preferred Stocks must have a Moody's credit worthiness rating of "investment grade." What do you think happens to the Moody's rating of a company that has a history of missing dividend payments? It goes down of course, way down. In many cases it falls below investment grade.

---

[4] See Appendix B: The CDx3 Special Report *"Prospectus For The Rest Of Us"* provides the keywords commonly used throughout the prospectus of a CDx3 Preferred Stock that describe key provisions.

Not only is the company required to catch up in the extraordinary event that they miss a dividend payment to you, the CDx3 Selection Criteria's "investment grade" requirement provides a bit of double protection.

#7 Be Issued By A U.S. Company

In addition to having a Moody's rating of "investment grade," having a 100% successful record of never suspending dividend payments and limiting ourselves to just the preferred stocks that have "cumulative" dividends, CDx3 Preferred Stocks are also issued by U.S. companies - no foreign issues.

I do not have any quarrel with foreign companies. Foreign companies make some of the best chocolate, pharmaceuticals and automobiles on the planet.

CDx3 Investors deserve the protections afforded to investors in U.S. securities. Sure, foreign countries have their own stringent securities laws, but how would you, as a non-citizen of those foreign countries, evaluate their enforcement?

Further, CDx3 Investors should have a lot of visibility to events affecting their investments – the bigger and brighter the light shining on the companies with whom you have invested your money the better.

How does that work with the foreign media and corporate reporting requirements (and in a language other than English)?

Foreign issues of preferred stocks are out. Too many questions for low risk CDx3 Investors.

#8 Non-Convertible Preferred Stocks

A convertible preferred stock is a preferred stock that can be converted to the issuer's common stock at a certain conversion ratio (as specified in the prospectus).

For every share of a convertible preferred stock that you own, you will receive x shares of the company's common stock upon conversion.

The timing of this conversion is generally under your control except in the case of mandatory convertible preferred stocks (where you must convert your shares to the issuing company's common stock on a date specified in the prospectus).

The CDx3 Selection Criteria eliminates convertible preferred stocks for three reasons:

1) There are too many unknowns associated with the future value of the issuer's common stock. Since the conversion ratio is generally fixed, but the market price of the common stock fluctuates, there is no way to know if this is a good deal or a terrible deal;

2) While the conversion is generally under the holder's control, the issuer can force conversion to happen under certain market conditions. Those conditions are unpredictable. Being subjected to this uncertainty is too much risk, and continually tracking these conditions is too much work, for CDx3 Investors; and

3) Once your preferred shares are converted to common shares, you are no longer "preferred." You give up your position of being in front of common stock shareholders for dividend payments once your preferred shares are converted to common shares.

Convertible preferred stocks introduce both uncertainty (risk) and work – two things that the CDx3 Selection Criteria are designed to minimize. Keep it simple, stick with the sure thing and avoid convertible preferred stocks.

#9 Online Prospectus Available

Earlier I showed you how to access the online prospectus of a preferred stock and do so for free using the SEC's EDGAR system.

The provisions provided in the prospectus of a CDx3 Preferred Stock are legally binding and require the issuing company to meet a wide variety of obligations.

While reading a prospectus is a bit onerous, with some practice you'll be able to pick out what matters. If you cannot even get your hands on the prospectus, the deal's off. We'll be buying a different preferred stock.

#10 Initial Share Value Of $25.00

When a new CDx3 Preferred Stock is created (see chapter 2) and becomes available to the public for purchase, its opening cost is $25.00 per share. Sometimes referred to as the "par value," this price is specified in the prospectus of a CDx3 Preferred Stock.

Some preferred stocks cost $100 at IPO, others $50. The custom-made preferred stocks that some banks sold to the U.S. Treasury as part of the Trouble Asset Relief Program (TARP) in 2008 had a par value of $1,000 per share.

But CDx3 Preferred Stocks cost $25.00 per share at IPO, which is, by far, the most common preferred stock share price. As a CDx3 Investor, you will appreciate the complexity that is removed from your CDx3 Portfolio by fixing this value at a constant amount - $25.

A preferred stock must meet all ten of these CDx3 Selection Criteria in order to be considered a CDx3 Preferred Stock.

These ten CDx3 Selection Criteria are specifically designed to support the three objectives of the CDx3 Income Engine - (1) maximize revenue while (2) minimizing risk and (3) minimizing work.

The following table shows how each of these three objectives are supported by the ten CDx3 Selection Criteria.

CDx3 Selection Criteria	Objective
1. Pay a fixed dividend rate at least 6.5%	Revenue Maximization
2. 60 months of dividends	Revenue Maximization
3. Pay dividends quarterly	Revenue Maximization
4. Moody's investment grade only	Risk Mitigation
5. Never suspended dividends	Risk Mitigation
6. Cumulative dividend obligation	Risk Mitigation
7. U.S. companies; no foreign issues	Risk Mitigation
8. Non-convertible preferred stocks	Risk Mitigation
9. Online prospectus available	Work Reduction
10. Share price of $25	Work Reduction

While new preferred stocks are introduced to the stock market continually, ones that meet the above CDx3 Selection Criteria historically come out at a rate of about one or two per month. This rate of introduction slowed during the Global Credit Crisis and the recession that has followed. But so did the rate of "calls" where companies retire older issues so there are always dozens of high quality issues for CDx3 Investors to pick from as we'll see later.

Appendix A provides a list of helpful websites, some of which are free while others request a fee. For CDx3 Investors who choose not to subscribe to the CDx3 Notification Service, you can use the resources provided in Appendix A to mine data from various websites (public and private), data services, the issuing companies themselves plus other sources and distinguish one type of preferred stock from another.

EIGHT

MANAGING THE RISKS

No discussion of an investment approach would be complete without saying a few words about risk and how to manage it.

People take risks every day:

- 42% of newly licensed 16 year old drivers get into a police-reported car accident every year; and

- 58% of licensed teenagers get into a police-reported car accident every year[1].

Think about those numbers. These accident rates make me want to bring my dog inside every time my neighbor's teenager reaches for the keys. And this is just the police-reported accidents. How often do you think teens get into a one-car accident and call the police? The real percentages are much higher. And yet people share the road with teen drivers every day; they take the risk.

All investments come with a certain amount of investment risk and CDx3 Preferred Stocks are no exception. There are risks. Lightning may, in fact, strike.

But there is much one can do to substantially reduce the risk of being struck - don't walk around holding a nine iron over your head

---

[1] Source: National Safety Council, *Injury Facts*

during a lightning storm; don't stand outside in an open field; get off that metal ladder. In other words, if the risk is known you can build a dome of risk protection and crawl inside of it.

Stay Inside Your Dome

The less investment risk you have, the easier it is to manage. The number one concern of preferred stock investors is, of course, the bankruptcy of the issuing company. The number two concern is that while the company survives, they stop paying your dividends.

While companies that issue CDx3 Preferred Stocks have merged over the years, there has never been a case of a bankruptcy. And there has only been one case of a missed dividend payment (CTZ-A, see footnote on page 68).

To protect the President of the United States, the Secret Service has what they call a virtual dome of protection. The center of the dome is always represented by the president's physical location; the dome moves accordingly, always.

CDx3 Investors can use this same concept to build their own dome of protection – a collection of complementary measures that, taken together, form a dome within which you invest.

The key to minimizing your investment risk with CDx3 Preferred Stocks is simple – stay inside your dome. And I'm about to show you how to do exactly that.

Use CDx3 Selection Criteria #4 Through #8

Half of the ten CDx3 Selection Criteria are designed to support the objective of minimizing investment risk:

✓ #4 - Be rated "investment grade" by Moody's Investors Service;

✓ #5 - Be issued by a company that has a perfect track record of never having suspended the dividend payments on a preferred stock;

✓ #6 - Have a "cumulative" dividend obligation;

✓ #7 - Be issued by a U.S. company; and

✓ #8 - Must not be convertible to common stock in the future.

These five risk mitigation components of the CDx3 Selection Criteria are cumulative; that is, to be considered CDx3 Preferred Stock quality, a company's preferred stock must meet all of these five criteria. So these criteria are layers of protection, one on top of the other, between you and risk.

Take Advantage Of Corporate Longevity

The CDx3 Selection Criteria do not specifically include or exclude preferred stock from companies that are of a certain age. There is no criteria that says anything like "...and the issuing company must have been in business since at least 1950..."

And yet, most of the companies that issue CDx3 Preferred Stocks are multi-billion dollar businesses that have been in business for decades.

As we'll see in Part IV regarding how you go about selling a CDx3 Preferred Stock, depending on market conditions those inclined to be sellers are usually only going to own a CDx3 Preferred Stock for about two or three years and some times less than one year.

The chances that these companies would be in business for decades and just happen to go bust during the precise sliver of time that you happen to own one of their preferred stocks is extremely slim to begin with.

Relative to the longevity of these businesses, you are going to be in and back out in a relative blink of the eye.

By applying each of these CDx3 Selection Criteria, your risk mitigation dome gets stronger and stronger. In the next section I will provide you with the Kevlar coating that will make your dome nearly bullet proof – simply, easily and for free.

Diversify Your CDx3 Portfolio

Decades ago preferred stocks were only issued by utilities, but now many types of businesses offer them allowing you to salt your portfolio with holdings from different segments of our economy.

- Utilities
- Self-storage units
- Insurance
- Commercial centers
- Retail shopping
- Shipping/logistics
- Hotels
- Apartments
- Regional Banks
- Broker/Banks

CDx3 Preferred Stocks provide an excellent opportunity to not only earn great dividend and capital gain income, but also diversify your portfolio at the same time.

This type of investment diversification allows you to take advantage of boom times and spread your risk during periods when the economy slows down.

For example, during stronger economic times the demand for the services of shipping and logistics centers ramps up as more goods are being moved around the world and hotels see more travelers.

When times are tighter, demand for apartments increases and self-storage units fill up.

Here is a breakdown of how these industries are represented among all of the CDx3 Preferred Stocks issued between January 2001 and December 2006 (pre-Global Credit Crisis)[2].

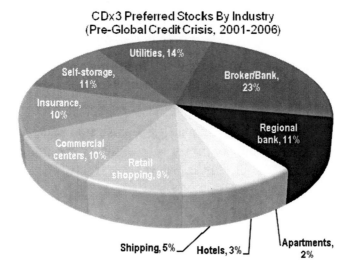

CDx3 Preferred Stocks By Industry
(Pre-Global Credit Crisis, 2001-2006)

It is also a good idea to read the Risks section of the prospectus of a preferred stock that you are considering purchasing. This section tends to read quite a bit like the potential side effects disclaimer on a prescription medication. Those who take the Risks section too literally will find themselves rarely investing in anything (or even going

---

[2] Cash strapped banks issued a number of preferred stocks during the crisis that distorted these percentages somewhat. The pre-crisis distribution presented here provides a more illustrative representation.

outside). So use your best judgment here and try not to read too much into these provisions.

And let's not forget why they are called "preferred" stocks to begin with – we get to stand in line before the holders of common stocks in the event of a cash crunch.

By combining (1) the excellent track record of the CDx3 Selection Criteria, even under the most extreme of economic circumstances, (2) the sliver of time that you will own a particular CDx3 Preferred Stock in relation to the longevity of the companies that can meet these criteria and (3) diversifying your CDx3 Portfolio across multiple industries, you can build a very powerful risk mitigation dome.

By using what you have learned so far in this chapter you will start to see which CDx3 Preferred Stocks are most consistent with your personal financial resources, goals and risk tolerance.

But what about actually measuring investment risk? In the next section I will show you an interesting analysis for quantifying the investment risk of CDx3 Preferred Stocks.

Quantifying Risk

CDx3 Selection Criteria number 4 requires that CDx3 Preferred Stocks be rated "investment grade" by Moody's Investors Service. The resulting rating by Moody's helps investors assess the investment risk associated with their investments.

But what about The Market itself? Generally, as perceived investment risk goes up so will the yield of that investment; that is, if The Market perceives that the investment risk is higher, the market price will tend to be lower in order to push investors to take that risk.

The problem with The Market is that buying and selling decisions made by investors are subject to emotion - fear or elation - while ratings imposed by Moody's Investors Service are not. So how do they compare? If prices are dropping there must be more risk, right? Is The Market always right?

The following analysis documents the difference in the conclusions that emotion-driven investors can reach regarding preferred stocks when compared to non-emotional analytics. I will use a collection of CDx3 Preferred Stocks as they were trading during the Global Credit Crisis since the difference we are trying to examine here was magnified under those extreme conditions and therefore much easier to see and measure.

While this analysis is not a part of the CDx3 Income Engine methodology (you will never find yourself having to do this), I think that you will find this analysis of a key aspect of the preferred stock marketplace to be very interesting nonetheless.

Risk As Assessed By The Market

The yield is your annual return, expressed as a percentage, on the money that you actually have invested in a CDx3 Preferred Stock (your purchase price).

In the case of CDx3 Preferred Stocks, if The Market views two issues as having identical risk, the yields of the two issues should be the same (or close to it), assuming everything else is equal.

One way to test this is to take two CDx3 Preferred Stocks from the same company that were issued at about the same time and compare their yields. If The Market is able to accurately assess investment risk of CDx3 Preferred Stocks we would expect the yields of two such CDx3 Preferred Stocks to be nearly identical.

One such example is provided by the twin CDx3 Preferred Stocks issued by Public Storage less than 90 days apart in October 2006 and January 2007.

PSA-L and PSA-M from Public Storage have dividend rates of 6.750% and 6.625%, respectively. And Moody's assigns the same level of risk to them—Baa1.

Since they have the same investment risk (according to Moody's), The Market should price them such that they provide the same return (as measured by their yield) to investors.

Looking up the market prices for PSA-L and PSA-M, I find (at this writing) that PSA-L is selling for $25.70 per share while PSA-M is selling for $25.38 per share.

Let's calculate the yield that these two "equal risk" CDx3 Preferred Stocks provide to investors who purchase them at these prices. Here is the formula for the yield of a CDx3 Preferred Stock:

Yield = ($25 times [declared dividend rate]) / [purchase price]

Plugging in our values for PSA-L and PSA-M we get:

Yield for PSA-L = ($25 times 6.750%) / $25.70 = 6.57%

Yield for PSA-M= ($25 times 6.625%) / $25.38 = 6.53%

The Market has priced PSA-L and PSA-M such that they have the same yield of about 6.5%.

So The Market and Moody's are in agreement; PSA-L and PSA-M are properly priced, given the risk.

Moody's Versus The Market

The extreme conditions of the Global Credit Crisis allow us to see where The Market and Moody's part company. So let's expand this analysis and compare a group of CDx3 Preferred Stocks that all ended their dividend quarters in December 2008. By using CDx3 Preferred Stocks that are at the same point in their respective dividend quarters,

I do not have to worry about the Rule of Buyer/Seller Behavior pressuring their market prices differently.

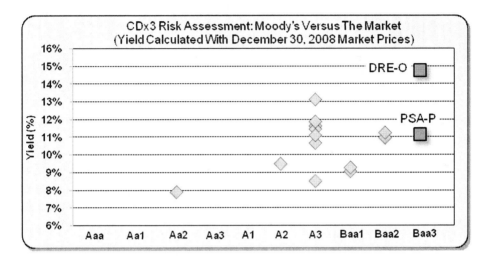

Remember, all CDx3 Preferred Stocks are investment grade. But this chart shows Moody's ten investment grade sub-categories from lowest to highest risk across the bottom.

If The Market has priced the CDx3 Preferred Stocks at a given risk level correctly, the diamonds that you see above that risk level should all be on top of, or very near, each other.

And notice that they are—with two exceptions: A3 and Baa3.

Look at how spread out the column of diamonds is above the Moody's A3 rating. At this level of risk, The Market is as confused as a rookie batter facing a veteran pitcher's curve ball.

Now look at the Moody's Baa3 rating. Moody's says that there are two CDx3 Preferred Stocks – DRE-O and PSB-P – at this level of investment risk in our sample[3].

---

[3] Moody's ratings as published on December 30, 2008. Source: *www.Moodys.com*

DRE-O was issued by Duke Realty on February 14, 2008 with a declared dividend rate of 8.375%. PSB-P is a CDx3 Preferred Stock from PS Business Parks and was issued on January 10, 2007 and pays a 6.7% annual dividend.

Since Moody's assigns both of these CDx3 Preferred Stocks the same investment risk The Market should, theoretically, price them such they provide the same yield.

But notice that the yield for DRE-O was substantially higher (14.7%) than the yield provided by PSB-P (11.1%).

This analysis tells us that either Moody's or The Market (or both) has blown the call. Either PSB-P was overpriced (producing a lower yield) or DRE-O was underpriced for the level of investment risk that Moody's is saying it represents.

But which is it? Is PSB-P overpriced or is DRE-O underpriced?

Identifying Mispriced CDx3 Preferred Stocks

To answer that question, we have to look at the market prices more closely. Given that these two CDx3 Preferred Stocks carry the same investment risk (according to Moody's), their yields should be much closer.

In December 2008, at the height of the crisis, the average annual yield being paid by CDx3 Preferred Stocks was about 10.8%. Since new CDx3 Preferred Stocks sell for a market price of about $25, we can draw a "constant yield line" on this chart showing a constant yield of 10.8%; just as a CDx3 Preferred Stock that pays 10.8% and sells for $25.00 yields 10.8%, so does a CDx3 Preferred Stock that pays a 6.5% dividend selling for a market price of $15.03.

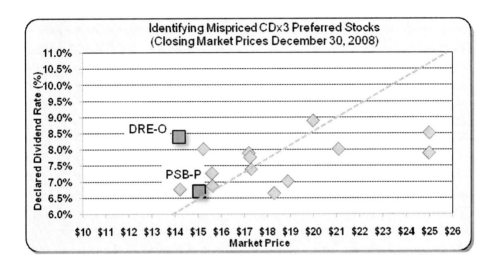

CDx3 Preferred Stocks that are found on, or close to, this constant yield line are those that The Market and Moody's agree on. The Market and Moody's are both assigning the same level of investment risk to these CDx3 Preferred Stocks.

Of our two CDx3 Preferred Stocks, you can see by the above chart that the investment risk associated with PSB-P is properly assessed by The Market; that is, since PSB-P falls on the constant yield line The Market and Moody's are in agreement regarding the investment risk of PSB-P.

DRE-O, however, is located well to the left of the constant yield line, implying that The Market feels that there is more investment risk associated with DRE-O than Moody's does. Remember, Moody's has assessed PSB-P and DRE-O at the same risk level of Baa3. If Moody's has assessed the investment risk of DRE-O properly then the market price of DRE-O should be about $19.50 rather than $14.18 on the day this data was collected.

What this analysis demonstrates is that The Market (influenced by emotion) and Moody's (which is not influenced by emotion) are not always in agreement when it comes to assessing the investment risk associated with CDx3 Preferred Stocks.

By using the CDx3 Selection Criteria and diversifying your CDx3 Portfolio across several industries you can form a dome of protection within which you invest at a level of risk that is acceptable to you.

So now you know how to identify new preferred stocks and use the ten CDx3 Selection Criteria to find the highest quality issues – CDx3 Preferred Stocks.

An update to the CDx3 Income Engine Summary Table is presented on the following page that illustrates the progress you are making.

CDx3 Income Engine Summary Table

	CDx3 MARKETPLACE DIRECTION	
	Buyer's Market	**Seller's Market**
HOW TO TELL (Part I)	▪ Dividend rates increasing ▪ Market prices < $25 per share ▪ CDx3 Perfect Market Index >100	▪ Dividend rates decreasing ▪ Market prices > $25 per share ▪ CDx3 Perfect Market Index <100
SELECTING (Part II)	▪ CDx3 Selection Criteria ▪ SEC EDGAR system ▪ Watchlist (one for each quarter) ▪ CDx3 Preferred Stock catalog	▪ CDx3 Selection Criteria ▪ SEC EDGAR system ▪ Watchlist (one for each quarter) ▪ CDx3 Preferred Stock catalog

BUYING (Part III)	▪ New issues > Over-The-Counter
	▪ CDx3 Bargain Table
	   - < $25 per share
	   - Early in dividend quarter
	   - Old issues > 2nd dividend qtr
	▪ Big Bank TRUPS
	▪ CDx3's Beyond Call Date
		▪ New issues > Over-The-Counter
		▪ CDx3 Bargain Table
		   - < $25 per share
		   - Early in dividend quarter
		▪ Big Bank TRUPS
		▪ CDx3's Beyond Call Date

SELLING (Part IV)	▪ Enjoy dividend checks; do not sell during a buyer's market ▪ Check for "upgrades"	▪ Market price > Target Sell Price; or ▪ Called by issuing company for $25 ▪ Last day of dividend quarter ▪ Check for "upgrades"

Now that you know how to pick out CDx3 Preferred Stocks from a sea of pretenders, let's see how to use the Three Rules of Market Price Predictability to buy CDx3 Preferred Stocks for less than $25 per share during different market conditions.

PART III
Buying When The Market Favors Buyers

I am very happy with the CDx3 method. I used to put my longer term money into CD's and government agency debt. Now I buy preferred stocks from the CDx3 Bargain Table. It's a perfect fit!
- Carl J., Subscriber

Never forget that five years after a CDx3 Preferred Stock is issued, the issuing company regains the right to purchase your shares back from you (a "call"). If they decide to do so they will pay you $25 for every share that you own.

Therefore, as a CDx3 Investor, you always want to purchase your CDx3 Preferred Stocks for less than $25 per share. By doing so, you know in advance that you are in line for a downstream capital gain (in the event of a call) plus above average dividends in the meantime.

Now I am going to show you how to use the Rule of Buyer/Seller Behavior and the Rule of Rate/Price Opposition to not only purchase your CDx3 Preferred Stocks for less than $25 per share, but do so at a point in time that tends to favor buyers regardless of economic conditions.

This Part of *Preferred Stock Investing* includes three chapters:

- ✓ Chapter 9 explains the process for buying *newly issued* CDx3 Preferred Stocks for less than $25 per share even when average CDx3 market prices are much higher;

- ✓ Chapter 10 deals with identifying and purchasing *previously issued* CDx3 Preferred Stocks using a special tool called the "CDx3 Bargain Table"; and

- ✓ Chapter 11 explains two specific buying opportunities available right now, both of which were caused by the Global Credit Crisis (the crisis that keeps on giving).

BUYING NEWLY ISSUED CDx3 PREFERRED STOCKS

Many preferred stock investors favor purchasing preferred stocks when they are first introduced to the marketplace since such issues usually have a longer dividend payout period than issues that have been trading for a while.

Also, since preferred stocks tend to attract long-term investors, the daily trading volume of older preferred stocks is often lighter when compared to that of newer issues. Shareholders intent on holding their shares until the preferred stock is retired are not actively trading so there are not as many sellers in the market each day of many older issues. Consequently, those looking to make a purchase often find that newly issued preferred stocks can be more convenient to buy.

As described in chapter 2, when a new preferred stock is issued to the marketplace the dividend rate is set such that there is a market for the new security at $25.00 per share.

But if you are never supposed to pay more than $25.00 per share when you purchase a CDx3 Preferred Stock, and new issues are always issued at $25, how in the world are you ever going to purchase shares of a new issue? This chapter is going to show you how.

Using The Over-The-Counter Stock Exchange

In October 2010 Public Storage introduced their Series P CDx3 Preferred Stock (PSA-P, 6.500%). PSA-P was introduced on October 6, 2010 but, as you can see on the below chart, if you were looking to purchase shares on the New York Stock Exchange (NYSE) you were not able to do so until October 12, six days later.

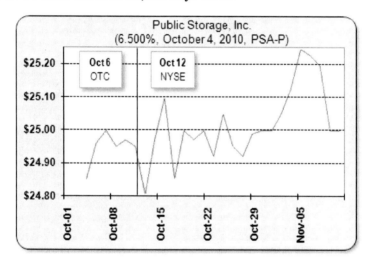

But obviously, looking at this chart, somebody was buying shares of PSA-P prior to October 12, 2010 and at pretty favorable pricing too.

What happened to PSA-P during these initial days, the time between its introduction (its IPO date) and the beginning of trading on the NYSE and who were these other investors who were able to buy the new shares?

It is during this phantom period, while newly issued CDx3 Preferred Stocks are "off the radar," that CDx3 Investors are able to purchase new CDx3 Preferred Stock shares for less than $25 per share. Here's how to do it.

Motivated Sellers

Typically when a new CDx3 Preferred Stock is issued it takes the New York Stock Exchange a bit of time (usually about two weeks, sometimes more, sometimes less) to approve the trading application filed by the issuing company and assign a trading symbol.

When a new CDx3 Preferred Stock is issued to the marketplace a group of underwriters provides the issuing company with the cash in exchange for the new shares. And we're not talking about small amounts of money here either; the underwriters are out real money usually measured in tens or even hundreds of millions.

Once the underwriters have purchased the new shares from the issuing company they are very anxious to turn around and sell those shares to the dealer/brokers who, in turn, sell them to you.

In other words, the holders of the shares at this point in the process, before the CDx3 Preferred Stock actually shows up on the NYSE, are what a real estate agent refers to as a "motivated seller." The underwriters are in no mood to simply sit and wait until the NYSE gets around to assigning a trading symbol; the underwriters want to sell the new shares to the dealer/brokers as quickly as possible and they are not going to wait for the NYSE.

To sell the new shares to the dealer/brokers as quickly as possible, the financial services industry invented a "pre-market" trading venue where new shares of CDx3 Preferred Stocks are bought and sold prior to transferring over to the NYSE. This pre-market is called the Over-The-Counter (OTC) stock exchange.

And the best part is that, in addition to the big guys, individual investors like you and me can trade on the OTC too[1].

---

[1] See Appendix B: CDx3 Special Report *"Trading Over-The-Counter."* This CDx3 Special Report is provided to new subscribers to the CDx3 Notification Service.

Swim With The Big Fish

When the underwriters buy the new shares from the issuing company, they receive a commission from the issuing company for their services of about 3%, so the net price per share paid by the underwriters for the new shares is usually about $24.25.

As the process unfolds, this $0.75 per share underwriter commission provides some wiggle room for discounts to downstream participants as the process continues to make its way to you and me.

When the underwriters sell the new shares to the dealer/brokers, the underwriters may set the wholesale price at, say, $24.50. At this price, the underwriters make a very quick $0.25 per share on what is usually several million shares for what is essentially a few hours of work and very little risk.

The dealer/brokers turn around and sell the new shares to investors like us. Depending on how quickly they want or need to unload the new shares, they might set their "ask" price at, say, $24.75.

With an online trading account, individual investors can access the OTC just like the big guys. By inserting yourself into the trading action on the OTC, you can usually purchase newly issued CDx3 Preferred Stocks for less than $25 per share.

By doing so, you are essentially taking a piece of the original underwriter's commission and putting it into your own pocket.

Once the shares make their way onto the NYSE and out into the open market the original underwriter's commission has usually been fully absorbed by the players in the pre-market and is no longer available after OTC trading.

Other Reasons For The Discounted OTC Prices

Beyond the underwriter and dealer/broker's need to sell the new shares quickly, there are two other reasons why CDx3 Investors can purchase a newly issued CDx3 Preferred Stock for less than $25.00 per share while it is trading on the OTC.

First, the visibility of the OTC is much lower than that of the major stock exchanges like the NYSE or NASDAQ exchange. Low visibility leads to low volume; lower volume leads to lower prices.

Secondly, the Rule of Buyer/Seller Behavior (page 45) tells us that there is upward pressure on the market price of a CDx3 Preferred Stock as the end of the dividend quarter (payday) approaches. That means that there is less upward pressure on the market price at the beginning of a dividend quarter, which is when new CDx3 Preferred Stocks are usually introduced.

Both of these lesser factors put downward pressure on the market price of a newly issued CDx3 Preferred Stock while it is trading on the OTC stock exchange.

Example: Entering An OTC Buy Order

The OTC is not as automated as the much higher volume major exchanges. In fact, part of the OTC process that your broker goes through (on your behalf) involves *manual* processing.

Consequently, a buy order that you enter for a CDx3 Preferred Stock trading OTC may take a little longer than you may be use to.

To help out, there is a third party involved called a "market maker." Only certain market makers handle certain preferred stocks on the OTC, so sometimes there can be delays between your broker, trying to place your buy order, and the market maker.

As illustrated on the following diagram of the OTC, the market maker is where your buy order is actually matched up with someone else's sell order and the deal is made.

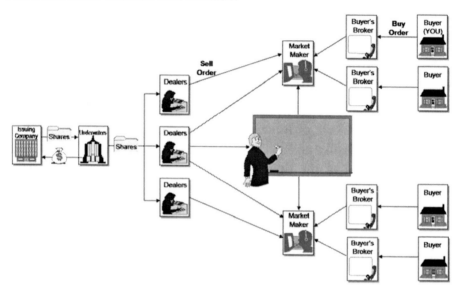

The market maker actually works the deal between your broker (representing you, the buyer) and the seller by telephone. The results are posted on an electronic bulletin board, but broker systems are limited with respect to how much of the bulletin board they have access to.

You should check with your broker (online brokerage or traditional brokerage) and ask them if they can process an "over-the-counter" preferred stock purchase. This should not be a problem but, as explained below, processing over-the-counter transactions is more cumbersome for your broker (not for you), whether they are an online or traditional brokerage. TDAmeritrade (www.TDAmeritrade.com), for example, has made a real commitment to handling OTC preferred stock transactions.

While being traded over-the-counter, a new CDx3 Preferred Stock will have a temporary trading symbol that is updated when it transfers to the NYSE. Once the NYSE approves the trading application, a new permanent trading symbol is assigned and any shares that you purchased under the temporary OTC symbol are transferred over automatically.

Here is an example of a buy order to purchase a CDx3 Preferred Stock while it was trading on the OTC using a brokerage account at TDAmeritrade.

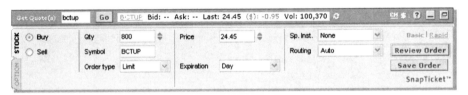

Note the temporary trading symbol BCTUP[2]. In this example, I am telling TDAmeritrade's system to tell the market makers with whom TDAmeritrade has contracts that I want to purchase 800 shares of BCTUP at any price up to $24.45 per share. And if they cannot do this deal by the end of the day, cancel my order.

Notice also that the Bid and Ask values are blank. Since broker systems have very limited electronic access to pending OTC trades, you will usually have to call your broker to get the current Bid and Ask prices for CDx3 Preferred Stocks while they are trading OTC. When you do so, your broker will put you on hold and call the market maker.

While buying a CDx3 Preferred Stock while it is trading OTC is not as automated as doing so from the NYSE, do not be deterred. Depending on market conditions, this may be the last time that your new CDx3 Preferred Stock will be available to you for a market price less than $25.00. Believe me; it's worth the phone call to your broker.

---

2 BCTUP was the temporary OTC trading symbol for BAC-C from Bank of America.

Because underwriters and dealer/brokers are very anxious to sell newly issued CDx3 Preferred Stock shares in order to recoup their investment quickly, you are able to use the Over-The-Counter stock exchange to purchase shares for a market price below $25, effectively taking a piece of the $0.75 per share commission out of the underwriter's pocket and putting into your own.

You now know how to buy newly issued CDx3 Preferred Stocks for less than $25 per share, even during a seller's market when average market prices exceed that value.

But what about previously issued CDx3 Preferred Stocks?

As I am writing this there are several dozen CDx3 Preferred Stocks available for less than $25 per share. Issues that were introduced within the last five years have not even reached their call dates yet. And, as I will explain in chapter 11, market conditions have not favored calls for several years now (another gift of the Global Credit Crisis) so the inventory of high quality preferreds is currently much larger than usual.

While the tables in chapter 15 identify CDx3 Preferred Stocks, you want to make sure that when making a purchase you are doing so at a time that tends to most favor buyers. Let's look at how to identify previously issued CDx3 Preferred Stocks that are at a point in time that makes them ripe for picking.

BUYING PREVIOUSLY ISSUED CDx3 PREFERRED STOCKS

Buying is the fun part. Any day that you buy a CDx3 Preferred Stock is going to be a good day because it is this day that you are giving yourself a well deserved raise.

Always remember that as a preferred stock investor you are paid based on the *number of shares* you own so any time you buy more shares your income goes up. That's a great day!

While the number of candidates moves up and down over time (largely depending on what interest rates are doing as I'll explain shortly), there are always dozens of CDx3 Preferred Stocks available to pick from.

In this chapter I am going to show you a simple method for not only identifying purchase candidates but we're going to go a bit further and narrow the list down to just the few issues that appeal to your individual investing goals as well.

Specifically, we are going to create what I call the "CDx3 Bargain Table." And you can follow the steps here at any time and the result will always be a list of the highest quality preferred stocks that not only meet your goals but are at a point in time that tends to favor buyers.

The CDx3 Bargain Table method of identifying specific purchase candidates works just as well whether interest rates are decreasing, stable or increasing. It is the length of the resulting list that will depend on what interest rates are doing so understanding what is likely to be happening with interest rates throughout the economy is as important as always.

Inflation And Interest Rates

On December 16, 2008 the Federal Reserve (the "Fed") delivered an enormous gift to preferred stock investors and in this chapter I am going to explain how you can take advantage of it by creating your own CDx3 Bargain Table.

The "federal funds rate," probably more than any other single interest rate, drives the cost of money throughout the U.S. economy. In addition to being the interest rate at which banks can borrow money for short-term loans, the federal funds rate impacts the yields offered by other fixed-income investments such as treasury bonds, corporate bonds, bank CDs and preferred stocks.

To help stimulate the economy (and achieve a few other policy objectives related to bank stabilization) the Fed lowered the federal funds rate to essentially zero percent in December 2008. At this writing in early 2011, that is still the case. Since December 2008 the U.S. economy has been in the ultimate "low interest rate environment."

There are three directions that interest rates can go – increase, remain the same or decrease. With the federal funds rate set near zero, we know for the first time in modern history that the direction of interest rates, going forward, is not going to be decreasing.

By keeping the federal funds rate so low, the Fed has eliminated one-third of the uncertainty that preferred stock investors face when contemplating the future direction of interest rates. When is the last time that a single fact eliminated one-third of the uncertainty you were facing while considering an investment opportunity?

The Fed's near-zero percent federal funds policy continues and many economists and analysts say it is likely to continue through 2012. In an early-2011 CNBC interview Jan Hatzius, chief U.S. economist at Goldman Sachs, stated "In terms of the level of interest rates, we still think that they will basically be at zero in 2011 and probably in 2012 as well."

Hatzius (and many others) base this view on the persistently high unemployment that has ravaged U.S. consumer spending for several years. Even with slightly improving employment numbers at the end of the first quarter of 2011, the number of unemployed U.S. workers is about double what it was in 2006, prior to the Global Credit Crisis and ensuing recession.

Inflation caused by consumer spending (as opposed to that caused by speculative spikes in oil or other commodity prices) is closely watched by the Fed and increasing the federal funds rate is the primary tool used to cut off inflation. Hatzius continued: "I find it hard to believe that we'll get higher inflation, broadly speaking, at a time when we have a [high] unemployment rate."

Without strong employment you cannot have strong consumer spending; without strong consumer spending you cannot have consumption-driven inflation; and without consumption-driven inflation, the Fed is very unlikely to start increasing the federal funds rate very aggressively.

So if it is not possible for the federal funds rate to go down (since it is currently at zero) and the absence of consumption-driven inflation makes it unlikely that the Fed will push the federal funds rate up by much if at all, the widely held expectation is that interest rates are likely to remain low and very stable for some time to come.

Consequently (and this is why I took you through this review of recent history), market prices for preferred stocks and other fixed-income securities, for the next year or two, are likely to remain relatively stable as well. But once rates head up (which they will have to do at some point since they cannot go any lower), market prices for fixed-income securities (bonds, preferred stocks) that were issued earlier when rates were lower are likely to fall, driving down the cost of acquiring additional preferred stock shares.

As I will show you in a moment, that means that preferred stock investors should be able to continue earning about 7% annual dividend yields from CDx3 Preferred Stocks (the highest quality available) plus look forward to even higher yields in the future.

Preferred Stock Versus Common Stock Investing

I occasionally receive email from investors who have experience investing in common stocks but are new to preferred stock investing. The most common mistake that new preferred stock investors make is that they try to apply common stock investing methods to making preferred stock investing decisions.

The pitfalls in doing so were never clearer than during the Global Credit Crisis when market prices were falling. Forgetting that preferred stocks pay their dividends based on the *number of shares* you own, too many preferred stock investors sold their shares and, by doing so, not only decimated their principal but eliminated their own income at the same time.

Preferred stock investors invest in preferred stocks in order to receive the great dividend income that these securities produce. Preferred stock dividends are paid to you based on the *number of shares* you own, not the current market price or the price you originally paid for those shares. *For a preferred stock investor, it is all about accumulating shares.*

Common stock investors, on the other hand, invest hoping for a big run up in market price; a common stock's value (today's market price) is the key metric for common stock investors (buy low, sell high). Unlike preferred stocks, the success of a common stock investment is based on market price.

The day will come when the Fed begins gradually raising interest rates once again (2012, 2013?) which will put downward pressure on preferred stock market prices.

Since your dividend income from your preferred stock portfolio is based on the *number of shares* you own, preferred stock investors use a period of falling market prices to accumulate shares for bargain prices.

If you are new to preferred stock investing, be careful not to execute your *preferred* stock investing strategy based on *common* stock thinking. Doing so will often lead you to a place you do not want to be.

Finding Bargains

The purpose of the CDx3 Bargain Table is not just to help you identify purchase candidates, but to find candidates that are at a specific point in time that tends to favor buyers.

Building a CDx3 Bargain Table will find such purchase candidates regardless if we are in a buyer's or seller's market for CDx3 Preferred Stocks. However, during buyer's market conditions (low prices) you will notice that the resulting list of candidates will be longer since more issues are selling for a market price less than $25 during a buyer's market.

Here's what to look for when building your CDx3 Bargain Table.

Less Than $25 Per Share

Since your CDx3 Bargain Table only includes preferred stocks that are selling for less than $25 per share, the number of preferred stocks on your table will tend to grow as interest rates rise and prices fall. Rising interest rates, such as those expected to occur in 2012 or 2013, will deliver more choices to preferred stock buyers at favorable share prices.

Just Beginning A New Dividend Quarter

For your CDx3 Bargain Table you are looking for high quality preferred stocks that are at a point in time that tends to favor buyers. This is where we can use the Rule of Buyer/Seller Behavior from page 45. A preferred stock that is closer to the end of its dividend quarter (payday) will tend to take on more value in the marketplace than an otherwise identical preferred stock that is further away.

That means that the market price of a CDx3 Preferred Stock that has just completed one dividend quarter and is now about 90 days away from its next payday will tend to be lower than it would be otherwise; preferred stocks that are beginning a new dividend quarter this month are at a point in time that tends to favor buyers.

So when you put together your CDx3 Bargain Table you want to include CDx3 Preferred Stocks that are beginning a new dividend quarter this month (not all CDx3 Preferred Stocks use the same quarterly schedule; see page 240).

Time saving tip: In chapter 7 I showed you how to use the U.S. Securities and Exchange Commission's online EDGAR system to identify CDx3 Preferred Stocks. As you do so, it will save you tons of time if you keep track of the dividend quarter used by each. The simplest way to do this is to create three "watchlists" for CDx3

Preferred Stocks, one for each dividend quarter (see an example of a watchlist that I created using TDAmeritrade's system on page 92).

When you are looking for CDx3 Preferred Stocks that are beginning a new dividend quarter, just pull up your watchlist that includes this month.

Not Likely Or Able To Be Called

A CDx3 Preferred Stock that is about to be called (retired) by its issuing company does not usually attract a lot of buyers since, once the shares are retired, the issuing company pays shareholders $25 per share and that's the end of that. There are no further dividend distributions past that point.

So *when market conditions favor calls*, your CDx3 Bargain Table should not include CDx3 Preferred Stocks that are beyond their respective call dates.

But if market conditions *do not favor calls*, CDx3 Preferred Stocks that have exceeded their call dates are just as much in play as those that have yet to reach their call dates and can be included in your CDx3 Bargain Table.

As described in chapter 14, whether or not market conditions favor calls of previously issued CDx3 Preferred Stocks depends largely on whether or not the issuing company can save money by issuing a new preferred stock today and using the proceeds to buy back the shares of the older issue. To save money with this "refinancing" maneuver, dividend rates from five years ago have to have been higher than they are today, otherwise current market conditions do not favor calls since there is no savings to be had by the issuing company (see page 210 for an example).

That's exactly the situation we have now (2011+). CDx3 dividend rates five years ago (2006) were very close to what they are today so, with the occasional exception, current market conditions do not favor calls (see chapter 11 for a detailed discussion regarding why calls of CDx3 Preferred Stocks are currently minimal and likely to stay that way for another year or two).

Two Quarters Old (Buyer's Market Only)

During a buyer's market, prices of previously issued CDx3 Preferred Stocks are falling (good news for buyers). Initially priced at $25 per share, a new CDx3 Preferred Stock's market price will often fall to more favorable pricing within the first two dividend quarters during such conditions.

During a buyer's market, my research shows that you will generally find very favorable pricing by considering CDx3 Preferred Stocks that are at least two dividend quarters old for your CDx3 Bargain Table.

If prices are increasing (seller's market), this is not a consideration.

Identifying Purchase Candidates

To summarize, for your CDx3 Bargain Table you are looking for CDx3 Preferred Stocks that meet the following conditions:

1) Are available for a market prices less than $25;

2) Are just beginning a new dividend quarter, the point in time when the Rule of Buyer/Seller Behavior tells us that the market price will tend to favor buyers;

3) If market conditions do not favor calls, include issues that have exceeded their call dates.; and

4) Are at least two quarters old (buyer's market only).

Here are the twenty CDx3 Preferred Stocks that met these criteria at the end of March 2011 (sorted by Moody's rating).

Sym	Moody's Rating	Call Date	Closing Market Price[1]
AMB-L	Baa2	06/23/2008	$24.89
AMB-M	Baa2	11/25/2008	24.47
KIM-F	Baa2	06/05/2008	24.63
MSJ	Baa2	02/01/2011	24.45
MSZ	Baa2	10/15/2011	24.28
ABW-A	Baa3	05/30/2007	24.92
BRE-C	Baa3	03/15/2009	24.40
BRE-D	Baa3	12/09/2009	24.25
CFC-A	Baa3	04/11/2008	24.77
DRE-M	Baa3	01/31/2011	24.59
DRE-N	Baa3	06/30/2011	24.99
FBF-M	Baa3	03/08/2007	24.98
PL-A	Baa3	09/25/2007	24.94
PLD-F	Baa3	11/28/2008	23.65
PLD-G	Baa3	12/30/2008	23.97
PSB-P	Baa3	01/17/2012	24.40
VNO-F	Baa3	11/17/2009	24.72
VNO-G	Baa3	12/22/2009	24.20
VNO-H	Baa3	06/17/2010	24.49
VNO-I	Baa3	08/31/2010	24.28

Since market conditions did not favor calls at the end of March 2011 this table includes CDx3 Preferred Stocks that have exceeded their call dates as well as those that have yet to reach their call dates. Please note that this list changes continually with market price and market conditions, but this is how it looked at the end of March 2011.

At the end of March 2011 these were the candidates that were most likely to be available at bargain basement prices.

---

[1] Closing market prices on March 31, 2011.

Notice that the table is sorted by Moody's rating. By definition, all CDx3 Preferred Stocks are rated "investment grade" by Moody's Investors Service. Moody's investment grade category has ten sub-categories as follows (strongest to weakest):

Aaa, Aa1, Aa2, Aa3, A1, A2, A3, Baa1, Baa2, Baa3

Using the Moody's rating as a proxy for investment risk helps to identify candidates that best fit your personal risk tolerance. Subscribers tell me that they will often draw a line at a Moody's rating that best represents their personal risk tolerance and just consider CDx3 Preferred Stocks that are at or above that Moody's rating.

Because all of our candidates are in the early days of a new dividend quarter, the Rule of Buyer/Seller behavior tells us that their market prices will tend to be relatively low.

By using the of Buyer/Seller Behavior we have now identified, out of 1,077 U.S.-traded preferred stocks, the twenty highest quality issues that were at a point in time that most strongly favored buyers on March 31 , 2011.

And all you had to do was pull up your March-June-September-December watchlist to see them.

Maximum Dividend Yield

The next step is to determine which one(s), if any, to purchase. Which CDx3 Preferred Stock candidate is the best fit for your personal financial goals, resources and risk tolerance?

Only you can answer that question. Different CDx3 Investors are going to have differing investment objectives. Some might want to steer their purchases toward the highest dividend income producers while others may favor longer-term capital gain opportunities, for example.

Let's add a couple of columns that will serve to identify the real bargains even further.

For those who favor dividend income, we can add a column that shows the declared dividend rate that each of our candidate CDx3 Preferred Stocks pays (found right on the cover page of the prospectus and also provided in chapter 15).

Once we have the declared dividend rate for each candidate, it is a very simple matter to calculate the "yield" discussed earlier (the return that you are making in dividend income on the money that you actually have invested) since we already have the current market price.

Here are our twenty candidates with columns showing their respective dividend rates and yields:

Sym	Moody's Rating	Call Date	Closing Market Price[2]	Declared Dividends (Div Rate)	Dividend Yield
AMB-L	Baa2	06/23/2008	$24.89	6.500%	6.529%
AMB-M	Baa2	11/25/2008	24.47	6.750%	6.896%
KIM-F	Baa2	06/05/2008	24.63	6.650%	6.750%
MSJ	Baa2	02/01/2011	24.45	6.600%	6.748%
MSZ	Baa2	10/15/2011	24.28	6.600%	6.796%
ABW-A	Baa3	05/30/2007	24.92	7.625%	7.649%
BRE-C	Baa3	03/15/2009	24.40	6.750%	6.916%
BRE-D	Baa3	12/09/2009	24.25	6.750%	6.959%
CFC-A	Baa3	04/11/2008	24.77	6.750%	**6.813%**
DRE-M	Baa3	01/31/2011	24.59	6.950%	7.066%
DRE-N	Baa3	06/30/2011	24.99	7.250%	7.253%
FBF-M	Baa3	03/08/2007	24.98	7.200%	7.206%
PL-A	Baa3	09/25/2007	24.94	7.250%	7.267%
PLD-F	Baa3	11/28/2008	23.65	6.750%	7.135%
PLD-G	Baa3	12/30/2008	23.97	6.750%	7.040%
PSB-P	Baa3	01/17/2012	24.40	6.700%	**6.865%**
VNO-F	Baa3	11/17/2009	24.72	6.750%	6.826%
VNO-G	Baa3	12/22/2009	24.20	6.625%	6.844%
VNO-H	Baa3	06/17/2010	24.49	6.750%	6.891%
VNO-I	Baa3	08/31/2010	24.28	6.625%	6.821%

Now we are really getting somewhere. If you are looking for the best dividend income performers, they have just been identified for you.[3]

You can see how your actual yield increases, when compared to the declared dividend rate, when the Rule of Rate/Price Opposition pushes the market prices of our candidates down below $25 per share.

---

[2] Closing market prices on March 31, 2011. See page 134 for yield formula.
[3] The results of this example are for illustration purposes only. Please do not take these results as recommendations to buy or not to buy. Always gather additional and current information regarding investment alternatives prior to investing.

Knowing the dividend yield is very important since this value, unlike the declared dividend rate, takes into account your purchase price. For example, look at CFC-A and PSB-P. Both of these CDx3 Preferred Stocks have the same investment grade rating (Baa3). CFC-A has a declared dividend rate of 6.750% compared to PSB-P's 6.700%. But because PSB-P's market price is sufficiently lower than CFC-A's ($24.40 versus $24.77, respectively), your dividend return (yield) is actually higher with PSB-P.

Those looking to maximize their dividend return would be better off with PSB-P than CFC-A even though CFC-A has a higher declared dividend rate.

This example shows you in black and white how just picking the CDx3 Preferred Stock with the highest declared dividend rate is not necessarily the best move for those looking for the highest dividend income performer.

Highest Capital Gain Opportunity

Beyond dividend income there are additional investment objectives that this table can help us with.

What if you are more interested in positioning yourself for the highest capital gain, rather than current dividend income? For this example I am going to show you how a CDx3 Investor can position themselves to take advantage of the Big Bank TRUPS opportunity described in the next chapter.

Remember, in the event that the issuing company of a CDx3 Preferred Stock "calls" the issue, you will receive $25.00 for every share that you own, regardless of your purchase price or the then-current market price.

For CDx3 Investors who are interested in a longer-term capital gain opportunity we can add a column to our CDx3 Bargain Table that shows the capital gain opportunity in the event that your "built-in buyer" (the issuing company) calls the issue and buys it back from you for a price of $25.00.

Sym	Moody's Rating	Call Date	Closing Market Price[4]	Declared Dividends (Div Rate)	Dividend Yield	Capital Gain (if called)
AMB-L	Baa2	06/23/2008	$24.89	6.500%	6.529%	$0.11
AMB-M	Baa2	11/25/2008	24.47	6.750%	6.896%	0.53
KIM-F	Baa2	06/05/2008	24.63	6.650%	6.750%	0.37
MSJ	Baa2	02/01/2011	24.45	6.600%	6.748%	0.55
MSZ	Baa2	10/15/2011	24.28	6.600%	6.796%	0.72
ABW-A	Baa3	05/30/2007	24.92	7.625%	**7.649%**	0.08
BRE-C	Baa3	03/15/2009	24.40	6.750%	6.916%	0.60
BRE-D	Baa3	12/09/2009	24.25	6.750%	6.959%	0.75
CFC-A	Baa3	04/11/2008	24.77	6.750%	6.813%	0.23
DRE-M	Baa3	01/31/2011	24.59	6.950%	7.066%	0.41
DRE-N	Baa3	06/30/2011	24.99	7.250%	7.253%	0.01
FBF-M	Baa3	03/08/2007	24.98	7.200%	7.206%	0.02
PL-A	Baa3	09/25/2007	24.94	7.250%	7.267%	0.06
PLD-F	Baa3	11/28/2008	23.65	6.750%	7.135%	**1.35**
PLD-G	Baa3	12/30/2008	23.97	6.750%	7.040%	1.03
PSB-P	Baa3	01/17/2012	24.40	6.700%	6.865%	0.60
VNO-F	Baa3	11/17/2009	24.72	6.750%	6.826%	0.28
VNO-G	Baa3	12/22/2009	24.20	6.625%	6.844%	0.80
VNO-H	Baa3	06/17/2010	24.49	6.750%	6.891%	0.51
VNO-I	Baa3	08/31/2010	24.28	6.625%	6.821%	0.72

Where ABW-A might catch the interest of those looking for dividend income, PLD-F would be worth considering for those seeking to position themselves for a nice capital gain in the event of a call.

---

[4] Closing market prices on March 31, 2011. See page 134 for yield formula.

   www.PreferredStockInvesting.com

Even though PLD-F's dividend yield is lower than some of the others, its capital gain opportunity is much higher ($1.35 per share).

Which one you invest in, if any, gets back to your personal goals, resources and risk tolerance. But I think that you can see how this simple table is able to identify the real bargains for you.

Through the iterations of this table, we have seen how those who favor dividend income can quickly identify their strongest candidates.

Similarly, by adding the last column, CDx3 Investors who favor longer-term capital gain opportunities can see their best choices.

But what about CDx3 Investors who want the best of both worlds?

Best Overall Return

By looking at the above table, can you spot the top two CDx3 Preferred Stocks that, in the event of a call on their call date, offer the highest overall return?

As first described on page 100, the "effective annual return" of an investment considers (1) the declared dividend rate, (2) your purchase price and (3) the number of dividend payments that you will receive before selling on the sell date.

Once calculated for each of our candidates (using Excel's RATE function)[5], the effective annual return will show us the CDx3 Preferred Stocks that will produce the highest overall return on our investment. If you sell the CDx3 Preferred Stock prior to the call date for a higher price than $25.00, your effective return will be even higher.

The CDx3 Bargain Table identifies the CDx3 Preferred Stocks that are most likely to offer strong financial performance for CDx3 Investors who have varying investment objectives.

---

[5] See Appendix B: The CDx3 Special Report *"Calculating Your Rate Of Return"*

At the end of March 2011, the average interest rate being paid by a bank Certificate of Deposit was 1.499%[6]. Now take a look at the last column that I just added on the far right of the CDx3 Bargain Table on the next page. Compare the Effective Annual Return column to the Declared Dividend rate column. The Effective Annual Return column shows you in black and white the strength of the CDx3 Income Engine.

For the purposes of calculating the effective annual return I have used the call date as the sell date for those CDx3 Preferred Stocks that have yet to reach their respective call dates. For Big Bank TRUPS that are beyond their call dates, I used January 1, 2013 for the sell date which is the effective date of section 171 of the Wall Street Reform Act (see chapter 11). For all others, I also used January 1, 2013 as the sell date for comparability.

Using the Rule of Buyer/Seller Behavior to make your purchases at a point in time that tends to favor buyers, and do so for a market price less than $25.00 per share, adds a layer of capital protection and positions you for a downstream capital gain in the event of a call while generating respectable dividend income in the meantime.

---

[6] 24-months, $10k; source: *bankrate.com.*

CDx3 Bargain Table

(Ending March 2011)

Sym	Moody's Rating	Call Date	Closing Market Price[7]	Declared Dividends (Div Rate)	Dividend Yield	Capital Gain (if called)	Eff.Ann. Return (if called)
AMB-L	Baa2	06/23/2008	$24.89	6.500%	6.529%	$0.11	6.942%
AMB-M	Baa2	11/25/2008	24.47	6.750%	6.896%	0.53	8.308%
KIM-F	Baa2	06/05/2008	24.63	6.650%	6.750%	0.37	7.778%
MSJ	Baa2	02/01/2011	24.45	6.600%	6.748%	0.55	8.200%
MSZ	Baa2	10/15/2011	24.28	6.600%	6.796%	0.72	**13.246%**
ABW-A	Baa3	05/30/2007	24.92	7.625%	**7.649%**	0.08	8.055%
BRE-C	Baa3	03/15/2009	24.40	6.750%	6.916%	0.60	8.495%
BRE-D	Baa3	12/09/2009	24.25	6.750%	6.959%	0.75	8.897%
CFC-A	Baa3	04/11/2008	24.77	6.750%	6.813%	0.23	7.518%
DRE-M	Baa3	01/31/2011	24.59	6.950%	7.066%	0.41	8.204%
DRE-N	Baa3	06/30/2011	24.99	7.250%	7.253%	0.01	7.622%
FBF-M	Baa3	03/08/2007	24.98	7.200%	7.206%	0.02	7.449%
PL-A	Baa3	09/25/2007	24.94	7.250%	7.267%	0.06	7.605%
PLD-F	Baa3	11/28/2008	23.65	6.750%	7.135%	**1.35**	10.550%
PLD-G	Baa3	12/30/2008	23.97	6.750%	7.040%	1.03	9.660%
PSB-P	Baa3	01/17/2012	24.40	6.700%	6.865%	0.60	10.448%
VNO-F	Baa3	11/17/2009	24.72	6.750%	6.826%	0.28	7.649%
VNO-G	Baa3	12/22/2009	24.20	6.625%	6.844%	0.80	8.897%
VNO-H	Baa3	06/17/2010	24.49	6.750%	6.891%	0.51	8.255%
VNO-I	Baa3	08/31/2010	24.28	6.625%	6.821%	0.72	8.681%

Whether you are looking for high current dividend income, a longer-term capital gain opportunity or the strongest overall return in the event of a call, the CDx3 Bargain Table identifies the strongest candidates for your consideration.

---

[7] Closing market prices on March 31, 2011.

During the low interest rate environment that has prevailed since December 2008 (the heart of the Global Credit Crisis), companies have been able to raise capital by issuing very low interest rate corporate bonds so there have been fewer new preferred stocks issued than normal.

With fewer new issues to pick from, the CDx3 Bargain Table has taken on increased importance since it exposes the bargains that are available right now in the sea of existing preferred stocks.

The Global Credit Crisis, while nerve wracking at times, produced the highest returns in history for CDx3 Investors (see pages 234 and 235 for crisis-era results).

And low interest rates are but one aspect of the crisis that has persisted. The crisis also spawned two specific opportunities for preferred stock investors that I will explain in the next chapter. These are opportunities that are available to you right now (2011 – 2012).

After you read chapter 11 you will see why I refer to the Global Credit Crisis as "the crisis that keeps on giving."

ELEVEN

THE CRISIS THAT KEEPS ON GIVING

In addition to the continuing opportunities that are identified by the monthly CDx3 Bargain Table discussed in the previous chapter, there are two specific additional opportunities that will play out over the next two years that preferred stock investors should be aware of.

Both opportunities were caused by the Global Credit Crisis (what I think of as "the crisis that keeps on giving"). The first involves high quality trust preferred stocks issued by Big Banks (assets greater than $15 billion). The second opportunity facing us can be attributed to the Federal Reserve's continued low interest rate policy converging with a coincidence that exists between the market for high quality preferred stocks as it existed in 2006 and 2007 and today's market for these same types of securities.

The crisis the keeps on giving...and it is not done yet. Let's look at these two crisis-caused opportunities one at a time.

Big Bank Trust Preferred Stocks (TRUPS)

In response to the Global Credit Crisis, the Wall Street Reform Act became law in July 2010 establishing a variety of new rules for U.S. banks and creating an enormous opportunity for risk-adverse preferred stock investors for at least the next couple of years.

As I am about to explain, this opportunity presents itself with two groups of CDx3 Preferred Stocks – the first group includes trust preferred stocks issued by Big Banks (assets great than $15 billion) that are callable prior to January 1, 2013; the second group includes Big Bank TRUPS that become callable after that date.

As explained in chapter 2, there are three types of preferred stocks - traditional preferred stock, trust preferred stock (TRUPS) and third-party trust preferred stock. Most preferred stocks issued by banks over the last several years are TRUPS. An amendment to the Wall Street Reform Act by Senator Susan Collins that ultimately became section 171 of that law includes a subtle provision (by reference) that creates a great opportunity for preferred stock investors.

Banks are required to keep a certain amount of capital in reserve to cover the bank's risk (such as the likelihood that borrowers will default on their loan payments). Regulators use a variety of metrics, referred to as capital ratios, to measure how much capital a bank has on hand (as a percentage of its total assets).

One such capital ratio is called "Tier 1 Capital" and includes the bank's equity (common stock as well as preferred stock) but not the bank's debt (such as bonds issued by the bank). Prior to the Act, TRUPS were considered by regulators as a type of preferred stock (equity) so the value of a bank's TRUPS counted in the Tier 1 Capital calculation. By issuing a TRUPS, a bank was therefore able to boost its Tier 1 Capital metric into the land of respectability.

But under the Wall Street Reform Act, beginning January 1, 2013, the value of a bank's TRUPS will no longer be able to be included in the calculation of the bank's Tier 1 Capital.

While the Act does not require Big Banks to call their TRUPS, the Act eliminates the primary reason that these Big Banks issued these

TRUPS to begin with – the ability to include their value toward their Tier 1 Capital reserves.

That substantially increases the likelihood that these Big Bank TRUPS will, in fact, be called starting on January 1, 2013 with the group that is callable by that date and then followed by the rest as they reach their respective call dates. The Act's phase in period of three years following January 1, 2013 was designed to capture all then-current Big Bank TRUPS call dates as they existed when the Act became law in July 2010.

Remember, if you hold shares of one of these TRUPS when the bank calls it, you are going to receive $25.00 per share that you own, regardless of the then-current market price and regardless of your original purchase price. $25 per share; that's what you are going to get in the event of a call.

Many of the affected Big Bank TRUPS are regularly available for a market price below $25 per share[1]. If a TRUPS is eventually called by its issuing bank, investors who purchased their shares for less than $25 will receive a nice capital gain, on top of the great dividend income that their shares will earn in the meantime.

Thanks to Senator Susan Collins, we know the specific preferred stocks involved; we know their exact call date; we know their current market price and we know the price that we will sell them back to the issuing bank for on that date in the event of a call.

And in that event, we know what our capital gain income is going to be and the day that we will receive it. And we know what our dividend income is going to be in the meantime and the date each quarter that we will receive that income.

---

[1] Six such issues can be seen on the CDx3 Bargain Table on page 167: MSJ, MSZ, ABW-A, CFC-A, FBF-M and PL-A.

When is the last time you knew all of this about an investment that you were considering?

Not only do we know all of this, but, unlike most other investments, we know it in advance.

Using the CDx3 Bargain Table criteria established in the previous chapter, here is a table identifying the high quality preferred stocks that (1) are TRUPS, (2) are issued by Big Banks, (3) are just starting a new dividend quarter (as of March 31, 2011) and (4) are currently selling for a market price less than $25 per share.

Big Bank Trust Preferred Stocks
(Ending March 31, 2011)

Sym	Moody's Rating	Call Date	Closing Market Price[2]	Declared Dividends (Div Rate)	Dividend Yield	Capital Gain (if called)	Eff.Ann. Return (if called)
MSJ	Baa2	02/01/2011	24.45	6.600%	6.748%	0.55	8.200%
MSZ[3]	Baa2	10/15/2011	24.28	6.600%	6.796%	0.72	8.654%
ABW-A	Baa3	05/30/2007	24.92	7.625%	7.649%	0.08	8.055%
CFC-A	Baa3	04/11/2008	24.77	6.750%	6.813%	0.23	7.518%
FBF-M	Baa3	03/08/2007	24.98	7.200%	7.206%	0.02	7.449%
PL-A[4]	Baa3	09/25/2007	24.94	7.250%	7.267%	0.06	7.605%

For Big Banks that call their TRUPS under the Act, these six specific preferred stocks should be among the first to deliver a capital gain to their owners plus earn an average annual dividend yield of about 7% in the meantime.

---

[2] Closing market prices on March 31, 2011.

[3] This table assumes no calls until January 1, 2013.

[4] In January 2009 the Federal Reserve approved Protective Life (PL) as a bank holding company.

The far right column on the above table shows you how adding a capital gain to the remaining dividend payout pushes your Effective Annual Return (EAR) up substantially, courtesy of the Wall Street Reform Act. Expect this list of purchase candidates to get shorter as January 1, 2013 approaches and buyers push market prices of these issues toward $25 per share in anticipation of a call.

A word of caution here: I think you can see by the above list that Big Bank TRUPS can offer an appealing buying opportunity for preferred stock investors. Just remember that this list changes continually since it includes TRUPS that are selling below a certain market price ($25) and were just starting a new dividend quarter on March 31, 2011 when this data was gathered. Be sure to update this information before considering an investment.

Not too interested in purchasing bank-issued preferred stocks? No problem. Let's look at the second opportunity that the Global Credit Crisis has provided to preferred stock investors.

Investing Beyond The Call Date

Remember that CDx3 Preferred Stocks that have exceeded their respective call dates can be "called" (retired) by the issuing company at any time, the shareholders receiving $25.00 per share in that event.

Preferred stock investors are long-term investors. Purchasing a preferred stock only to have it called by the issuing company a few days or weeks later is something that preferred stock investors generally seek to avoid.

Historically, preferred stock investors will therefore look to newer preferred stocks to make their purchases (chapter 9 explains how to purchase new preferred stocks for a discount). That is, preferred stock investors tend to stay away from preferred stocks that have exceeded their respective call dates, especially under conditions that The Market believes favors calls.

But what of preferred stocks that have exceeded their call dates that The Market does *not* believe are likely to be called?

We will explore why companies call preferred stocks and how to tell if conditions favor them doing so in chapter 14. Most commonly though, if a company can save money by issuing a new CDx3 Preferred Stock today at a low dividend rate and use the proceeds to call (buy back from you) an older higher dividend rate issue, they will usually do so. But today's rates have to be lower than rates were five years ago in order for this to work; otherwise, calls are unlikely (more on this later).

The Market has not believed that conditions favor calls since 2008. This means that almost all CDx3 Preferred Stocks that have been issued since 2003 are still available for preferred stock buyers.

Here's what happened. The Global Credit Crisis created a big bubble of high dividend rate preferred stocks in 2008, right when CDx3 Preferred Stocks issued during 2003 (with dividend rates around 7%) were reaching their five year call dates.

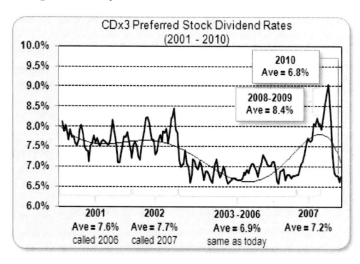

The crisis pushed the going dividend rate for CDx3 Preferred Stocks up and over 9%, shutting off calls of previously issued CDx3 Preferred Stocks. Issuing a new preferred stock at 9+ percent in order to call a 2003 issue that was only costing the company 7% makes no sense. So, while CDx3 Preferred Stocks issued during 2001 and 2002 have almost all been called, issues introduced since then have not due to the timing of the Global Credit Crisis.

While the current low rate environment would normally spawn a good number of calls, the crisis blocked calls of 2003 and 2004 issues. By the time 2005/06 issues became callable in 2010/11, CDx3 dividend rates had come back down to 2005 levels eliminating calls of 2005/06 issues as well.

Consequently, almost all of the CDx3 Preferred Stocks issued since 2003 continue to be available to preferred stock buyers.

And we are not likely to see a significant increase in the number of calls until the high dividend rate crisis-era CDx3 Preferred Stocks start to become callable in late-2012.

Since market conditions are unlikely to favor calls over the next couple of years (with the exception of Big Bank trust preferred stocks in response to the Wall Street Reform Act as described earlier in this chapter), preferred stock investors should not fear a scenario where a preferred stock is purchased only to be called a few days, weeks or months later.

While we will still see the occasional call, preferred stocks that meet all other CDx3 Selection Criteria but are currently beyond their respective call dates are just as worthy of consideration as those that have yet to reach their call dates.

When calls are unlikely, preferred stock investors can substantially increase the number of purchase candidates that are entirely worthy of consideration by including preferred stocks that have exceeded their respective call dates.

The average dividend yield offered by such high quality preferred stocks on March 31, 2011 was 6.962%; this at a time when the average 24-month bank CD pays an annual interest rate of less than 2%.

The crisis that just keeps on giving.

This Part of *Preferred Stock Investing* has focused on identifying purchase candidates from the sea of 1,000 to 2,000 preferred stocks that trade on U.S. stock exchanges every day.

You learned how the Over-The-Counter stock exchange works and how to use it to purchase *newly issued* CDx3 Preferred Stocks for less than $25 per share, even when average preferred stock market prices are much higher.

Chapter 10 showed you how to identify the highest quality *previously issued* preferred stocks that are available for a market price less than $25 per share at a point in time that tends to favor buyers. Using real data from March 31, 2011 as an example, we produced the CDx3 Bargain Table that identified the top twenty candidates.

And this chapter described two specific opportunities that are facing preferred stock investors over the next year or two – Big Bank TRUPS and a large number of CDx3 Preferred Stocks that have exceeded their respective call dates – courtesy of the Global Credit Crisis.

The CDx3 Income Engine Summary Table presented on the following page has now been updated. The row that summarizes how to buy CDx3 Preferred Stocks, both during a buyer's market and a seller's market, is now complete.

CDx3 Income Engine Summary Table

	CDx3 MARKETPLACE DIRECTION	
	Buyer's Market	**Seller's Market**
HOW TO TELL (Part I)	▪ Dividend rates increasing ▪ Market prices < $25 per share ▪ CDx3 Perfect Market Index >100	▪ Dividend rates decreasing ▪ Market prices > $25 per share ▪ CDx3 Perfect Market Index <100
SELECTING (Part II)	▪ CDx3 Selection Criteria ▪ SEC EDGAR system ▪ Watchlist (one for each quarter) ▪ CDx3 Preferred Stock catalog	▪ CDx3 Selection Criteria ▪ SEC EDGAR system ▪ Watchlist (one for each quarter) ▪ CDx3 Preferred Stock catalog

BUYING
(Part III)
	▪ New issues > Over-The-Counter
	▪ CDx3 Bargain Table
	  - < $25 per share
	  - Early in dividend quarter
	  - Old issues > 2nd dividend qtr
	▪ Big Bank TRUPS
	▪ CDx3's Beyond Call Date
		▪ New issues > Over-The-Counter
		▪ CDx3 Bargain Table
		  - < $25 per share
		  - Early in dividend quarter
		▪ Big Bank TRUPS
		▪ CDx3's Beyond Call Date

SELLING (Part IV)	▪ Enjoy dividend checks; do not sell during a buyer's market ▪ Check for "upgrades"	▪ Market price > Target Sell Price; or ▪ Called by issuing company for $25 ▪ Last day of dividend quarter ▪ Check for "upgrades"

So far we have covered how to tell the direction of the marketplace for CDx3 Preferred Stocks (Part I), how to select the highest quality preferred stocks from a sea of pretenders (Part II) and how to purchase CDx3 Preferred Stocks at a point in time that tends to favor buyers (Part III).

In the next Part of *Preferred Stock Investing* we will move on to selling CDx3 Preferred Stocks, adding a nice downstream capital gain to the above average dividend income that you've been earning in the meantime.

PART IV

Selling When The Market Favors Sellers

Prior to subscribing to the CDx3 Notification Service, I was very much struggling to better understand what determined the prices of preferred stocks. I have been so impressed with your service.

- Mark T.

If you decide to just hang on to your CDx3 Preferred Stocks and enjoy the great dividend income, that's your business.

But if the market price increases to a point where it may be worth selling, this Part of *Preferred Stock Investing* explains how to do so at the right time. Specifically:

- ✓ Chapter 12 explains how to avoid getting stuck with a low paying preferred stock that you can never sell;

- ✓ Chapter 13 describes how to know if you are better off by holding on to a CDx3 Preferred Stock or by selling it using the Target Sell Price as a guide;

- ✓ Chapter 14 shows you how an approaching call date can affect your investing decisions. Research is presented here that allows you to assess the likelihood that your CDx3 Preferred Stock will be called; and

- ✓ Chapter 15 presents the investing results for every CDx3 Preferred Stock that has been issued since January 2001 for those who have used the CDx3 Income Engine as described throughout this book.

TWELVE

ADDING CAPITAL GAINS TO GREAT DIVIDEND INCOME

Over the last several chapters you have learned how, when and where to purchase CDx3 Preferred Stocks during various market conditions. And always for less than $25 per share.

As soon as you purchase a CDx3 Preferred Stock, the CDx3 Income Engine starts sending dividend income your way at a steady pace. For "traditional" preferred stock investors, that's good enough. Since the dividend rates paid by CDx3 Preferred Stocks range from 6.5% to 9%, just cashing the nice quarterly dividend checks meets the goals of many individual investors.

Think about that. The least rate of return that you can expect to receive on a CDx3 Preferred Stock is the declared dividend rate. And that's if you purchase your shares at $25.00 per share.

Remember, since the dividend is based on a $25 share value, your return (your yield) is actually higher than the declared dividend rate when you purchase your shares for less than $25 as you learned to do in Part III.

The below chart shows the average annual yield that you would have earned had you purchased every CDx3 Preferred Stock[1], using the methods described throughout Part III, that has been issued since January 2001.

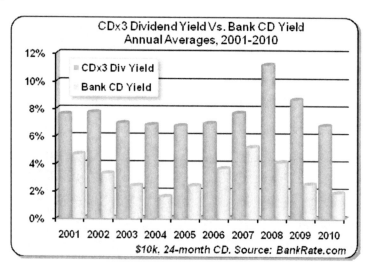

As illustrated by this chart, the dividend yield paid by CDx3 Preferred Stocks, before we even talk about the possibility of adding a downstream capital gain, is substantially higher than the interest rates earned by bank CDs.

You'll have to decide if the lower investment risk associated with bank CDs is worth the lower income opportunity that this chart makes clear. But I think knowing what the exact difference is can be an important piece of information to have when making that decision.

The traditional advice given to preferred stock investors is to buy them for the nice quarterly dividend and ignore the fluctuations in

---

[1] See chapter 15 for an itemization by year of the investment results for each CDx3 Preferred Stock.

market price. If you're not planning on selling your preferred stock, what difference does it make whether the current market price is higher or lower than the price you paid some time ago?

Richard Young, who has been publishing a very successful investment newsletter for over 20 years, puts it this way:

> "Preferreds trade like long bonds, meaning values fall in an environment of advancing long-term interest rates. Pay no attention to volatility in values on your brokerage statement. You are investing simply for a flow of cash to spend or to compound. That's it. Forget capital gains.[2]"

While I generally agree with Mr. Young's conservative investment approach, he and I part company on this point.

Many investors cannot stand to pass up a significant money making opportunity, especially when it requires next to no extra time, effort or risk. "Forget capital gains." I don't think so; not when I can double my money by taking them at the right time. Leaving this kind of money on the table goes against the primary objective of the CDx3 Income Engine – maximize revenue.

I used to be a "traditional preferred stock investor" until I realized that I could double my money (or more) by selling at the right time and for no more time or effort than I was already expending. At that point, the opportunity to take the capital gains got pretty hard to ignore.

Subscribers to the CDx3 Notification Service include both types – traditional preferred stock investors (buy and hold) as well as those looking to sell downstream and add a capital gain onto their earnings. All subscribers use the CDx3 Buyer's Notification email messages and preferred stock catalogs while those looking for a downstream capital gain are also interested in the seller's resources.

---

[2] Richard Young's *Intelligence Report*, May 2006

It's up to you, but walking away from the capital gain, when all you have to do is check the market price of your CDx3 Preferred Stock *once per quarter*, can be hard to do.

Never Sell At A Loss

The first objective of the CDx3 Income Engine is to maximize your revenue. Never sell at a loss. As I am about to explain throughout this chapter, with CDx3 Preferred Stocks there is no need to.

In Part III you learned how to always purchase your CDx3 Preferred Stocks for a market price below $25 per share. For market prices to exceed $25 and deliver a capital gain opportunity to you, dividend rates of new issues have to fall below the declared dividend rate of your CDx3 Preferred Stock (dividend rates down, market prices up – the Rule of Rate/Price Opposition).

Falling dividend rates and increasing market prices create a seller's market for CDx3 Preferred Stocks and that's when CDx3 Investors consider selling for a nice capital gain.

Let The Seller's Market Come To You...

As illustrated by the chart on page 79, by watching the yield rate on the five-year Treasury note over a long period of time we can see how frequently the direction changes from increasing to decreasing and back again.

You might have to hold onto a CDx3 Preferred Stock for a year or two or even longer[3], but the Rule of Rate/Price Opposition will guarantee that when rates fall again (and they will) the market price of such a CDx3 Preferred Stock will come back up.

---

[3] Refer to the "Sell Date" column presented in the results tables in chapter 15.

You do not want to sell during a buyer's market when market prices are low; that's when you buy dividend-generating shares for great prices and build your CDx3 Portfolio as explained throughout Part III.

Relax, be patient and let the seller's market come to you.

While you are waiting for dividend rates to change direction, just keep cashing the quarterly dividend checks.

...But Stay Off The Bottom

I receive email messages from CDx3 Investors who, before they knew better, purchased a low (below 6.5%) dividend paying preferred stock some years ago for about $25 and have yet to see a selling opportunity. They wonder if they are going to be stuck with these low payers forever with no chance for a downstream capital gain.

This is where CDx3 Selection Criteria number 1 comes in. In addition to meeting the other nine CDx3 Selection Criteria (see chapter 7), to be considered a CDx3 Preferred Stock, a regular preferred stock must have a declared dividend rate of at least 6.5%.

Preferred stocks historically offer dividend rates between 6% and 9%[4]. By putting a floor at 6.5% for CDx3 Preferred Stocks, CDx3 Investors will be spared the case where, over any five year period, they purchase CDx3 Preferred Stocks "at the bottom."

While there is nothing wrong with a 6.0% dividend, when dividend rates come back up off of 6.0%, holders of 6.0% issues will often find themselves unable to sell them without a capital loss.

That is, as dividend rates rise above 6%, market prices for those 6% preferred stocks will tend to fall below $25 (the Rule of Rate/Price

---

[4] This range covers about 95% of the investment grade, cumulative, fixed-rate preferred stocks issued since 1940.

Opposition again) and will stay there until dividend rates come back down to 6% some day.

Just as preferred stock dividend rates rarely reach 9%, they rarely fall all the way to 6% either. So if you purchase a preferred stock at 6%, you are likely to be holding onto it for quite a while.

By building in a .5% cushion, CDx3 Investors are always holding CDx3 Preferred Stocks that carry a selling opportunity over time (if a downstream capital gain is an objective).

When dividend rates fall below 6.5%, holders of CDx3 Preferred Stocks that pay 6.5% or higher will find themselves holding CDx3 Preferred Stocks with market values that tend to be greater than $25, which creates a capital gain opportunity (remember, the CDx3 Income Engine stipulates that you always purchase for a market price less than $25).

If you ever expect a capital gain, you cannot get into a situation where you hold preferred stocks that pay at the bottom of the scale, below 6.5%.

Putting in a floor at 6.5% helps to save this from happening to you as a CDx3 Investor.

In late-2006 and into early-2007, for example, the dividend rates being offered by many investment grade preferred stocks fell below 6.5%, pushing the market prices of CDx3 Preferred Stocks with 6.5% declared dividend rates above $25.

CDx3 Investors who owned CDx3 Preferred Stocks C-U and USB-I, for example, both with declared dividend rates of 6.5%, were able to sell them in December 2006 and January 2007 for $25.45 and $25.58, respectively.

Upgrading – Trade In A Low Payer For A Higher Payer

There is nothing wrong with purchasing 6.5% CDx3 Preferred Stocks as long as you do so while rates are stable or falling. Avoid it while rates are rising if you are expecting a capital gain in the near-term.

And be prepared to sell your newly purchased 6.5% CDx3 Preferred Stock fairly quickly, too. As rates bounce off of 6% and head back up your selling opportunities will diminish as the rising rates push market prices down again.

In March 2011 there was a lot of concern in the financial press that inflation would be upon us soon and that the Federal Reserve would have no choice but to start increasing interest rates in order to cool things off. Since the Fed has held the federal funds rate at near-zero since December 2008, this speculation about increasing interest rates has produced an interesting opportunity for preferred stock investors; an opportunity that we have not seen with any consistently for some time.

By using a technique called "upgrading," a preferred stock investor is able to trade in a low dividend paying preferred stock for a higher payer and have cash left over. Upgrading opportunities usually present themselves during periods of stable or increasing rates.

Using data from the end of March 2011, let's see how it's done. The below table appeared in the April 2011 issue of the subscriber's newsletter *CDx3 Research Notes,* making subscribers aware that upgrade opportunities were starting to appear in the marketplace.

IPO Date	Symbol	Preferred Stock Name	Div Rate	Last Price	Moody's
6/16/2006	DRE-N	Duke Realty Corp , 7.25% Dep Shares Series N Cumul.	7.25%	$24.97	Baa3
11/03/2006	CFC-B	Countrywide Capital V, 7.00% Capital Securities	7.00%	$24.92	Baa3
7/27/2006	BAC-C	BAC Capital Trust XII, 6 7/8% Capital Securities	6.875%	$24.85	Baa3
8/24/2010	KIM-H	Kimco Realty Corp , 6.90% Dep Shares Cumul Redeem ...	6.90%	$24.82	Baa2
10/08/2010	PSB-R	PS Business Parks, 6.875% Dep Shares Cumul , Series .	6.875%	$24.65	Baa3
1/10/2007	PSB-P	PS Business Parks, 6.70% Dep Shares Cumul , Series.	6.70%	$24.49	Baa3
2/16/2007	HPT-C	Hospitality Properties Trust, 7.00% Series C Cumul.	7.00%	$24.35	Baa3
10/06/2006	MSZ	Morgan Stanley Capital Trust VII, 6.60% Capital Securities	6.60%	$24.13	Baa2
1/24/2007	WRI-F	Weingarten Realty Investors, 6.50% Dep Shares Cumul.	6.50%	$23.78	Baa3

This table is a screen image taken on March 30, 2011 from the Preferred Stock List™ software tool available to subscribers. The list is sorted by Last Price (market price). In this list of nine CDx3 Preferred Stocks trading for less than $25 per share, there are five upgrade opportunities. Can you spot them?

You can produce this list yourself by using the watchlists that I described in chapter 10. Pull up your watchlist of CDx3 Preferred Stocks and sort by the last trade price (which is the same as the current market price). Then follow these steps to find upgrade candidates.

Here's the trick: a table with no upgrade candidates, once sorted by Last Price, will also show the Div Rates in sorted order, highest to lowest. But notice that this is not the case here. The Div Rate column starts out okay—7.25% to 7.00%, 7.00% to 6.875%; so far, so good. But then, after BAC-C's 6.875%, the next Div Rate is higher. We go from BAC-C's 6.875% up to KIM-H's 6.90%.

Bingo. We have found our first upgrade candidate. If you own shares of BAC-C, which pays 6.875%, you could sell them for $24.85 and use the proceeds to buy KIM-H, which pays a higher 6.90%, and have $0.03 per share in cash left over. That's upgrading.

Here are the five upgrade opportunities from the above list.

	SELL			BUY			RESULTS	
	Sym	Div Rate	Price	Sym	Div Rate	Price	Div Gain	Cash Gain
1	BAC-C	6.875%	$24.85	KIM-H	6.900%	$24.82	0.025%	$0.03
2	BAC-C	6.875%	24.85	HPT-C	7.000%	24.35	0.125%	0.50
3	KIM-H	6.900%	24.82	HPT-C	7.000%	24.35	0.100%	0.47
4	PSB-R	6.875%	24.65	HPT-C	7.000%	24.35	0.125%	0.30
5	PSB-P	6.700%	24.49	HPT-C	7.000%	24.35	0.300%	0.14

Each of these five upgrades involves trading in one CDx3 Preferred Stock for another and each opportunity produces gains to both your dividend income and cash position.

Look down the Results columns (far right) and notice how different upgrades can appeal to different investors.

Those seeking to maximize their dividend income would find upgrade number 5 appealing since it improves your dividend gain by .300%. Alternatively, investors looking to maximize their cash position would focus on upgrade number 2 since it improves your cash position by $0.50 per share.

Upgrading provides a mechanism for preferred stock investors to trade in their lower dividend paying preferred stocks for higher payers and have cash left over. Also, if you have low dividend rate preferred stocks in your portfolio that you'd like to upgrade, look for opportunities to do so whenever a new CDx3 Preferred Stock is introduced. The tables in chapter 15 show several examples of doing so.

Two Chances To Sell For A Capital Gain

As the Rule of Rate/Price Opposition explains, as dividend rates swing up and down over time, preferred stock market prices tend to move right along with them but in the opposite direction.

During a seller's market (market prices above $25 per share), you are going to have two opportunities to sell for a nice capital gain if you choose to be a seller:

1) Selling for the Target Sell Price; or

2) Selling to your "built-in buyer."

As chapter 13 will explain, the Target Sell Price calculation helps you answer the often-asked question "am I better off selling now and taking a capital gain or holding and collecting more dividend income?"

If you choose to forego selling and taking the capital gain, your next selling opportunity will come from the issuing company itself. If market conditions favor a call and the issuing company buys your shares back from you at $25 per share once the call date has arrived, you will have collected more dividend income (since you did not sell earlier for the Target Sell Price), but your capital gain will be less than it would have been.

A seller's market is all about deciding how much money you want to make and how quickly you want to make it.

Chapter 14 shows you how to determine the likelihood that the issuing company of your CDx3 Preferred Stock will call your shares once the call date arrives.

Which of these two capital gain opportunities to take advantage of (if at all) is, of course, up to you.

But because you know from the previous chapters how to purchase newly issued or previously issued CDx3 Preferred Stocks for a market price less than $25.00, there will come a day when you are staring at a nice capital gain if you sell. You're going to have a decision to make.

The following two chapters explain these two selling opportunities – selling for your Target Sell Price and selling to your built-in buyer.

THIRTEEN

SELLING FOR THE TARGET SELL PRICE

The Target Sell Price, as you are about to learn, helps answer the question: "Am I better off selling my preferred stock now for a capital gain or holding onto my shares longer and collecting more dividend income?"

The answer, of course, depends on the price that you can sell your shares for. But at what market price are you better off by selling rather than holding?

Answering that question can be a real hair-puller so let's look at an example.

In chapter 3 I described a scenario where you paid $25.00 for a single share of a fictional CDx3 Preferred Stock that pays an 8% dividend ($0.50 per quarter).

Since by selling to me at $25.49 the day before the ex-dividend date (the last day of the dividend quarter), you will miss out on any downstream capital gain, not to mention all future quarterly dividends, why on earth would you sell to me for a measly *one* quarter's worth of dividend cash?

Answer: You wouldn't. You'd also want to be compensated for the future capital gain opportunity and dividend income that you'd be giving up.

During a seller's market (when dividend rates are *decreasing* and market prices have exceeded $25 per share), sellers of CDx3 Preferred Stocks can demand up to *four* quarters worth of bonus revenue. More than that and you are going to miss out on some great prices; less than that and you're leaving money on the table.

In our fictional example, you would ask me for not $25.49, but for $27.00 ($25 + (4 x $0.50)).

Now we all know that market prices are not going to increase forever. There will come a time when dividend rates start increasing again and market prices start heading back toward $25. As long as market prices are still above $25, however, we are still in a seller's market (since you always purchase your CDx3 Preferred Stock shares for less than $25).

But as prices weaken (but are still above $25 per share), sellers of CDx3 Preferred Stocks must lower their expectations and will find themselves only able to demand three, two or even only one quarter's worth of bonus revenue.

Calculating The Target Sell Price

So the number of quarters worth of bonus revenue that you can demand when selling a CDx3 Preferred Stock depends on the strength of the seller's market.

Target Sell Price:

During a seller's market the Target Sell Price that you would be looking for on the last day of each quarter (when market prices tend to peak due to the Rule of Buyer/Seller Behavior) is calculated using the following formula:

$25 + ([number of bonus quarters] x [quarterly dividend amount])

We'll get to the calculation of the number of bonus quarters later in this chapter. Once you know the Target Sell Price of your CDx3 Preferred Stock, it is now a matter of continuing to collect your quarterly dividend checks until the market price exceeds the Target Sell Price.

When To Look For The Target Sell Price

But wait. One of the three objectives of the CDx3 Income Engine is to minimize work. No one wants to spend their days staring at their computer screen, watching the market price of your CDx3 Preferred Stock with your computer mouse carefully poised on the sell button.

This is where the Rule of Buyer/Seller Behavior (page 45) takes the work out of selling CDx3 Preferred Stocks. The Rule of Buyer/Seller Behavior tells us that the market price of a CDx3 Preferred Stock will tend to increase as the last day of the dividend quarter approaches (the day prior to the quarterly ex-dividend date).

Because of the Rule of Buyer/Seller Behavior, if you want to know if the market price of your CDx3 Preferred Stock has exceeded its Target Sell Price you only need to check the market price on the last day of the dividend quarter.

If you're not going to be around on the last day of the dividend quarter you can just tell your broker to sell if the market price exceeds the Target Sell Price or you can use the trade trigger[1] feature of your online trading account.

The rest of the time, enjoy your golf game.

I will discuss how to set the number of bonus quarters when calculating the Target Sell Price of a CDx3 Preferred Stock in a moment. But first, let's look at an example and see how you would have calculated the Target Sell Price and how you would have done when you sold a real CDx3 Preferred Stock.

Duke Realty (NYSE: DRE) is a $3.6 billion Real Estate Investment Trust (REIT) founded in 1972 and headquartered in Indianapolis. The company offers leasing, property and asset management, development, construction, build-to-suit, and other tenant-related services. Duke's properties include 139 million square feet of industrial, office and medical office properties in eighteen major U.S. cities.[2]

On February 14, 2008, DRE issued a CDx3 Preferred Stock paying an 8.375% annual dividend under the trading symbol DRE-O. DRE-O has a call date of February 22, 2013.

In February 2008 CDx3 dividend rates were increasing so the number of bonus quarters value for DRE-O was 2 quarters of bonus revenue (more on this in a moment).

---

[1] Most online brokerages, such as TDAmeritrade, provide the capability to set up a trade trigger in advance. You specify the trading symbol of the CDx3 Preferred Stock that you want to sell and the market price that you want to sell at. The system automatically monitors the daily market price for you and creates a sell order automatically if the market price hits the amount you specified. Several subscribers to the CDx3 Notification Service tell me that they set up trade triggers by setting the sell price to the Target Sell Price.

[2] As of December 31, 2010. Source: *www.dukerealty.com*

With an annual dividend rate of 8.375%, you will earn $0.523 per quarter for every share of DRE-O that you own. Using the formula for the Target Sell Price presented earlier, your Target Sell Price for DRE-O is therefore $26.05 ($25 + (**2** x $0.523)).

Below is a table that shows the closing price of DRE-O on the last day of each dividend quarter (the day that the quarterly "peak price" is most likely to occur) once the market had recovered in 2010 and once again favored sellers.

Qtr Starts On Ex-Dividend Date	Qtr Ends On Day Prior To Next Ex-Dividend Date	Market Price On Quarter Start Date	Looking For Target Sell Price	Market Price On Quarter End Date
Dec 15, 2009	Mar 12, 2010	$ 24.19	$ 26.05	$ 25.81
Mar 15, 2010	Jun 11, 2010	$ 25.29	$ 26.05	$ 25.44
Jun 14, 2010	Sep 13, 2010	$ 25.15	$ 26.05	$ 26.24
Sep 14, 2010	Dec 14, 2010	$ 25.60	$ 26.05	$ 26.36
Dec 15, 2010	Mar 14, 2011	$ 25.80	$ 26.05	$ 26.82

Notice that you can see the quarterly saw tooth pattern from page 49; the market price of DRE-O increases each quarter then drops as a new quarter begins (the Rule of Buyer/Seller Behavior in action).

On the day prior to each of these quarterly ex-dividend dates, when the Rule of Buyer/Seller Behavior is most likely to push up the market price to its peak for the quarter, you check the market price of DRE-O to see if it meets or exceeds your Target Sell Price of $26.05.

Looking at the above table, at the end of the first quarter, on March 12, 2010, you would have seen that the market price was $25.81. This is less than your Target Sell Price of $26.05. So, as a CDx3 Investor, you would not have sold on that date.

The same happens when you check the market price of DRE-O for the next quarter ending June 11, 2010. No sale yet since the market price on the last day of the June 2010 quarter ($25.44) is less than the Target Sell Price that you are looking for.

Qtr Starts On Ex-Dividend Date	Qtr Ends On Day Prior To Next Ex-Dividend Date	Market Price On Quarter Start Date	Looking For Target Sell Price	Market Price On Quarter End Date
Dec 15, 2009	Mar 12, 2010	$ 24.19	$ 26.05	$ 25.81
Mar 15, 2010	Jun 11, 2010	$ 25.29	$ 26.05	$ 25.44
Jun 14, 2010	Sep 13, 2010	$ 25.15	$ 26.05	**$ 26.24**
Sep 14, 2010	Dec 14, 2010	$ 25.60	$ 26.05	$ 26.36
Dec 15, 2010	Mar 14, 2011	$ 25.80	$ 26.05	$ 26.82

Three months later on September 13, 2010 you once again check the market price of DRE-O looking for your Target Sell Price of $26.05.

Looking at the above table, your Target Sell Price presents itself on that date, about a year and a half after DRE-O was introduced in February 2008. The price on that day, in fact, not only hits your $26.05 Target Sell Price, but blows right past it to $26.24.

How would you have done on your investment in DRE-O? As described in chapter 10, if you were following the method described there for buying your shares, you would have made your purchase on June 12, 2008 (the first trading day after the second dividend quarter) for $24.90 per share[3].

Selling your shares on the last day of the September 2010 dividend quarter (peak market price for the quarter), you would have earned $3.66 in dividends plus collected $1.34 in capital gain for a total gain of

---

[3] Dividend rates were increasing when DRE-O was introduced. See page 158 regarding buying after the second dividend quarter for more favorable prices.

$5.00 per share. That's an effective annual rate of return of 11.72% on your original $24.90 investment.

Here's the closing price chart for DRE-O from January 2010 through March 2011.

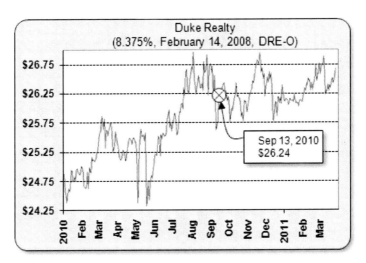

As the market continued its recovery from the Global Credit Crisis throughout 2010, investors eased back into the market, favoring the lowest risk alternatives (corporate bonds and high quality preferred stocks) first, driving up prices. The X symbol on the above chart is September 13, 2010, the day that the market price of DRE-O exceeded its Target Sell Price on the last day of a dividend quarter.

While you could have sold for a higher price at other times, doing so would have required continual monitoring of DRE-O's market prices breaking the third objective of the CDx3 Income Engine, minimize work. By following the Rule of Buyer/Seller Behavior, you captured a great price on September 13 and only had to check the market price once every three months.

By the way, in February 2008, if you had purchased a 24-month CD instead of this CDx3 Preferred Stock, your annual return would have been about 3.7%[4]. The CDx3 Income Engine returned about triple (3.1 times) what you would have earned had you invested in that CD rather than buying DRE-O.

Determining The Number Of Bonus Quarters

In chapter 3 I explained a concept known as the time value of money. It is the time value of money that makes the Target Sell Price, and its "number of bonus quarters" parameter, work.

For example, let's say you own a preferred stock that pays an 8% annual dividend; that's $0.50 per share per quarter in dividend income to you. As long as you own your shares when the market opens on the morning of the ex-dividend date, you are going to receive $0.50 per share from the issuing company.

But what if you could sell your shares the day before the ex-dividend date (when the market price tends to most favor sellers) for $2.00 per share more than your original purchase price? Pocketing a $2.00 per share capital gain is a whole year's worth (four quarters) of dividend income that you can receive right now in one shot.

$2.00 per share now or $2.00 per share spread out over the next year; which would you choose?

Many investors would rather have the money sooner rather than have the same money later (the time value of money – sooner is better). And that's why the Target Sell Price formula is structured the way it is.

Here is the formula for the Target Sell Price again:

---

[4] 24-month average U.S. bank CD APY. Source: *BankRate.com*

Target Sell Price = ($25 + ([number of bonus quarters] x [quarterly dividend amount]))

Notice that this formula adds some number of quarter's worth of dividend income to the "par value" of a preferred stock ($25 in our case). The number of quarter's worth of dividend income is what I refer to as the "number of bonus quarters."

There are two factors to consider when setting the number of bonus quarters parameter of the Target Sell Price calculation: (1) the competitive position of the CDx3 Preferred Stock when compared to others that are being issued at the time and (2) the direction of dividend rates. After explaining how this works I'll show you a table that allows you to set the number of bonus quarters with ease.

Competitive Position

CDx3 Preferred Stocks that pay a higher dividend will tend to command a higher market price. We would therefore assign a higher number of bonus quarters value to higher dividend payers which, in turn, would result in a higher Target Sell Price.

But there is a bit more to it than that. Investors, especially large institutional investors such as pension fund managers, also consider the remaining dividend payout potential of a preferred stock.

A CDx3 Preferred Stock that has a larger remaining payout potential tends to take on more value than one that is closer to its call date, even if the older issue has a somewhat higher dividend rate.

The competitive position of a CDx3 Preferred Stock is therefore only meaningful when compared to its peers (those of similar age and, therefore, with a similar remaining dividend payout).

So when we assign the number of bonus quarters value we do so at the time of introduction when the issue is new and compare its dividend rate to its other relatively new peers issued at about the same time. Such groups of peer CDx3 Preferred Stocks live their life in the marketplace together and compete directly for investor dollars until they are retired.

CDx3 Preferred Stocks of similar age that offer higher dividend rates have a stronger competitive position and will receive a higher number of bonus quarters value than weaker peers.

Direction Of Dividend Rates

When dividend rates are *decreasing*, there is upward pressure on market prices so you can command a higher price (i.e. raise the number of bonus quarters); when dividend rates are *increasing*, there is downward pressure on market prices so you will have to lower your expectations (i.e. lower the number of bonus quarters).[5]

The below table provides the number of bonus quarters depending on the competitive position of a CDx3 Preferred Stock you are considering and dividend rate direction.

Competitive Position	Rates Decreasing	Rates Stable	Rates Increasing
Best	4	4	3
Strong	4	3	2
Weak	3	2	1
Worst	2	1	1

---

[5] The investing results presented in chapter 15 use the direction of dividend rates as they existed at the time of introduction. Assessing dividend rate direction at the time of sale may produce a one quarter difference in the number of bonus quarters value in some cases but would involve a substantial amount of continuous effort since recalculating all Target Sell Prices would be required each time rate direction changes occur (breaking objective #3 of the CDx3 Income Engine – minimize work). Using the $25 par value in the Target Sell Price formula, rather than purchase price, mitigates much of this anomaly.

Example: 2003

Let's look at an example of how to use the above table to derive the number of bonus quarters. The following table lists the first five CDx3 Preferred Stocks introduced during 2003, a time when CDx3 dividend rates were *decreasing*.

Look at the dividend rates (third column) being offered by businesses up until early April 2003 when WRI-D and CFC-A were issued:

IPO Date	Sym	Div Rate	Quarterly Dividend	Number of Bonus Qtrs	Target Sell Price
02/03/03	RNR-B	7.300%	$ 0.46	4	$26.85
03/31/03	REG-C	7.450%	$ 0.47	4	26.86
04/04/03	WRI-D	6.750%	$ 0.42	3	26.27
04/08/03	CFC-A	6.750%	$ 0.42	3	26.27
04/08/03	NXL-E	7.625%	$ 0.48	4	26.91

A change in the dividend rate of 0.25% or more is considered significant. What were the financial gurus at Weingarten Realty Investors (WRI) and Countrywide Financial (CFC, since acquired by Bank of America) thinking? Talk about cheap. I understand that rates were declining at the time, but why the big rush?

If you bought these five CDx3 Preferred Stocks, you are obviously going to have a more difficult time selling WRI-D and CFC-A with their miserly dividend rates.

This is a clear case where you are not going to be able to demand the same premium (four quarters worth of bonus revenue) when you sell these two (WRI-D and CFC-A) that you can when you sell the others with their much higher dividend rates. For these two, we can probably get away with demanding *three* quarters of bonus dividend revenue, but certainly not *four*.

And if dividend rates were increasing when WRI-D and CFC-A were introduced (meaning downward pressure on market prices), you probably would have had to set your price expectations even lower – to one bonus quarter per the table we saw on the previous page.

If you are tracking CDx3 Preferred Stocks on your own you already have the information you need to determine the number of bonus quarters. The competitive position of new issues and the direction of dividend rates will be clear when you update your watchlist(s) of CDx3 Preferred Stocks (as explained on page 92).

So just by looking at the dividend rate on recent CDx3 Preferred Stock issues and your watchlist, you can use the table on page 202 to determine the number of bonus quarters for your CDx3 Preferred Stock. Plug that value into the formula on page 195 and you will have your Target Sell Price.

Am I better off selling now for a capital gain or continuing to hold and collecting more dividend income?

By understanding the effect that competitive position and dividend rate direction have on the market prices of CDx3 Preferred Stocks, we have now constructed a simple selling model (the Target Sell Price formula) that helps CDx3 Investors answer that question.

While Part III showed you how to purchase your CDx3 Preferred Stocks for a market price below $25 per share, you now know how to sell a CDx3 Preferred Stock for more than $25 per share using the Target Sell Price as a guide.

Looking at the tables in chapter 15, we see that there have been 158 CDx3 Preferred Stocks issued between January 2001 and December 2010. Of these, using the Target Sell Price would have resulted in the sale of 126 issues for an average effective annual return of 17.33%.

> **The CDx3 Income Engine**: Use the highest quality preferred stocks to earn above average dividend income while simultaneously creating multiple downstream capital gain opportunities.

You've just learned how to create one of those downstream capital gain opportunities by looking for the Target Sell Price on the last day of the dividend quarter (per the Rule of Buyer/Seller Behavior, page 45). Now let's look at selling your CDx3 Preferred Stock to your "built-in buyer," the issuing company itself.

FOURTEEN

SELLING TO YOUR 'BUILT-IN BUYER'

The CDx3 Income Engine produces respectable results by piling a capital gain on top of the above average dividend income you are earning in the meantime.

In the previous chapter you learned how to determine the market price at which you are probably better off by selling a CDx3 Preferred Stock rather than holding it – the Target Sell Price.

You also learned when the market price of a CDx3 Preferred Stock is most likely to reach, or exceed, the Target Sell Price during any given dividend quarter – the last day, per the Rule of Buyer/Seller Behavior (the day prior to the ex-dividend date).

But what if the Target Sell Price never presents itself or, even if it does, what if you're enjoying the dividend income so much you simply decided not to sell?

The CDx3 Income Engine provides you with two capital gain opportunities - (1) selling for your Target Sell Price on the last day of a dividend quarter (as described in the previous chapter) and (2) selling to your "built-in buyer" (the issuing company itself) when the call date arrives.

The opportunity to sell to your built-in buyer is where the Rule of Call Date Gravity (page 60) comes in; when market conditions favor a call, the market price of a CDx3 Preferred Stock will tend toward $25 as the call date approaches.

When Market Conditions Favor A Call

So how do you know if your CDx3 Preferred Stock is likely to be called by the issuing company or not?

To answer that question, we are going to use three of the ten CDx3 Selection Criteria:

- #1 – fixed-rate dividend;

- #2 – callable five years after IPO; and

- #10 - $25 par value

Because of these three CDx3 Selection Criteria you will be able to determine the likelihood that the issuing company of your CDx3 Preferred Stock is going to call (buy back from you at $25 per share) your shares.

The short answer is that the issuing company will tend to call your shares if it benefits them to do so. So the question really becomes, when's that?

Refinancing A CDx3 Preferred Stock

The likelihood of a call is directly related to the declared dividend rate of your CDx3 Preferred Stock. The higher the declared dividend rate, the more likely the call (once the call date arrives five years after its IPO date).

If the issuing company can save money by issuing a new CDx3 Preferred Stock at a lower dividend rate than your five year old issue, the issuing company is motivated to call your old CDx3 Preferred Stock.

For example, let's say you purchase a new CDx3 Preferred Stock that has a declared dividend rate of 8% and hold it for five years. If the "going dividend rate" five years from now is, say, 7% the issuing company of your now five year old CDx3 Preferred Stock can save 1% in annual dividend expense by issuing a new CDx3 Preferred Stock at 7% and using the proceeds to call (buy back from you) your old 8% shares.

The going dividend rate is just the declared dividend rate being paid by the most recently issued CDx3 Preferred Stocks.

By taking advantage of the fact that today's going dividend rate is lower than it was five years ago, the issuing company is able to "refinance" and save themselves a bunch of money.

Let's take a look at a real example of this refinancing mechanism in action.

 Public Storage, Inc. (NYSE: PSA) is a $19 billion California company founded in 1972. PSA operates over 2,100 locations in the United States and Europe, totaling more than 135 million square feet of net rental storage space.[1]

In April 2006, Public Storage issued a CDx3 Preferred Stock (PSA-I) with a 7.250% declared dividend rate.

Five years later in April 2011 the going dividend rate had dipped under 7%. That month the financial gurus at Public Storage filed with the U.S. Securities and Exchange Commission for a new preferred stock (PSA-Q) paying a dividend rate of 6.500% - 0.75% lower than their Series I preferred stock from five years earlier (PSA-I).

---

[1] As of December 31, 2010. Source: *publicstorage.com*

The "Use Of Proceeds" section of a prospectus will disclose what the issuing company intends on doing with the proceeds of a new preferred stock offering. The prospectus for the new PSA-Q says the following:

> "We estimate net proceeds from this offering of approximately $315.1 million, after all anticipated issuance costs. We expect to use the net proceeds from this offering to redeem depositary shares representing interests in our 7.25% Cumulative Preferred Shares, Series I at $25.00 per share..."

By issuing a new CDx3 Preferred Stock (PSA-Q) at 6.5% and using the proceeds to call PSA-I, Public Storage saved themselves several million dollars *per year* in dividend expense.

Not bad for just filling out a form and sending it to the SEC.

When CDx3 dividend rates are falling, there is an increase in demand from businesses to issue new preferred stocks (such as PSA-Q) in order to refinance their old higher dividend rate (7.250%) preferred stocks (PSA-I) at the new, lower rate (6.500%).

Consequently, the number of preferred stocks that are issued during a period of decreasing dividend rates tends to go up. There were 35 CDx3 Preferred Stocks issued during 2001, when rates were falling, compared to only 10 during 2008 when dividend rates were bid up by banks during the first full year of the Global Credit Crisis.

When rates are falling, you, as a buyer of CDx3 Preferred Stocks, will tend to have more new issues to pick from in part due to this refinancing mechanism[2].

---

[2] While common, issuing a new lower dividend paying preferred stock in order to generate the proceeds needed to call an older higher dividend paying issue is not the only option that the issuing company has when executing a call. Occasionally the issuing company will issue a bond (which typically carries a lower interest rate) in order to buy back an old higher dividend paying preferred stock. This approach, however, has limits since it converts equity (the preferred stock) into debt (the bond) on the company's books.

When Is It Enough?

In the previous example we saw how saving 0.75% in dividend expense was enough to tip the scales and motivate Public Storage to issue a new CDx3 Preferred Stock and use the proceeds to call (buy back from you at $25 per share) an older, higher paying issue.

With a 0.75% savings available, market conditions obviously "favored a call" (as the Rule of Call Date Gravity puts it).

But would Public Storage have called your shares of PSA-I if they could have only saved, say, 0.50% by doing so? What about if they could have only saved 0.25%, would your "built-in buyer" still have purchased your shares back from you?

In other words, where's the line? When is the savings enough to motivate the issuing company of a five year old CDx3 Preferred Stock to buy your shares back from you once the call date arrives? How much lower does the "going dividend rate" on the call date have to be than the declared dividend rate on your five year old shares for the issuing company to execute a call?

The answer is a scant .375% (3/8%). Less than one-half of a percentage point savings on the dividend rate is all it takes to motivate the issuing company of a CDx3 Preferred Stock to call a five year old CDx3 Preferred Stock when its call date arrives.

Can there be exceptions? Sure. But take a look at this data from CDx3 Preferred Stocks issued during 2001 when dividend rates were relatively high with many issues paying more than 8%.

Five years later, in 2006, the average CDx3 dividend rate was less than 7%, so there were savings to be had for issuing companies choosing to call their 2001 CDx3 Preferred Stocks on or near their 2006 call dates.

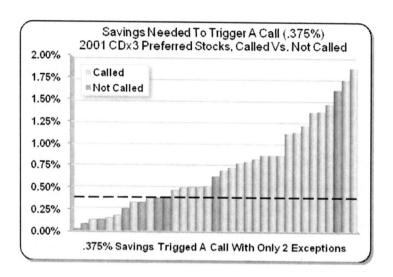

Savings Needed To Trigger A Call (.375%) 2001 CDx3 Preferred Stocks, Called Vs. Not Called

.375% Savings Trigged A Call With Only 2 Exceptions

Of the 12 CDx3 Preferred Stocks where the savings to the issuing company was less than .375% (3/8%), six were called and six were not.

But of the remaining 23 CDx3 Preferred Stocks issued during 2001 where the savings was greater than .375% to the issuing company, 21 (all but two) were called[3]. The next time these conditions will present themselves with such abundance will be in 2013 when the high dividend payers issued during the Global Credit Crisis (2008) become callable (see chart on page 174).

Likelihood Of A Call: The implication of this analysis is that when the issuing company of a CDx3 Preferred Stock can save at least .375% in annual dividend expense, there is a 91% chance that they will call the issue on or near its call date.

---

[3] Over time, variations in regulatory, commission and other costs can affect this value.

Market Price Behavior And The Call Date

The call date of a CDx3 Preferred Stock is the date, five years after IPO, that the issuing company regains the right to purchase your shares back from you at $25 per share. Whoever owns shares of the CDx3 Preferred Stock, once the call date arrives, is going to receive $25.00 per share – no more, no less – if the issuing company decides to call (buy back) the issue.

Since the call date of a CDx3 Preferred Stock is published in the prospectus, and all CDx3 Preferred Stocks have a $25 buy-back price in the event of a call, what do you think happens to the market price of a CDx3 Preferred Stock as the call date approaches?

If The Market believes that the issuing company is likely to call the issue, no one in the world is going to pay you much more than $25 per share as the call date approaches.

This, of course, is the foundation for the Rule of Call Date Gravity (see page 60).

In the previous section you learned how to tell if market conditions favor the call of a five year old CDx3 Preferred Stock. If the issuing company can save .375% on the dividend rate, they are very likely to issue a new CDx3 Preferred Stock (or bond) at the lower going rate (91% chance) and use the proceeds to buy the shares of the old CDx3 Preferred Stock back from you (at $25 per share).

If market conditions favor a call, the market price of your CDx3 Preferred Stock will tend to fall toward $25 like a rental horse heading back to the stable.

Approach From The North

Knowing that the market price of a CDx3 Preferred Stock will trend toward $25 as the call date approaches (if The Market believes a call is likely) can create an opportunity for CDx3 Investors (such as with the Big Bank TRUPS opportunity explained on page 169).

Many CDx3 Investors have asked if you could purchase an old CDx3 Preferred Stock that is approaching its call date for cheap (less than $25) thereby positioning you for a quick capital gain in the event of a call.

The answer is yes, but not because of anything new or mysterious.

Let me ask a question at this point: once the Rule of Call Date Gravity starts pulling the market price toward $25, do you think the market price will (a) fall toward $25, (b) rise toward $25 or (c) it depends on whether we're in a buyer's market or seller's market as the call date approaches?

The answer is (a). If market conditions favor a call, the market price of a CDx3 Preferred Stock will always *fall* toward $25 (approach from the north).

The market price of a CDx3 Preferred Stock that The Market believes is likely to be called will first tend to rise above $25, then fall back toward $25 as the call date approaches.

Here's why.

The Rule of Call Date Gravity will start to affect the market price of a CDx3 Preferred Stock as soon as it starts to look like market conditions are going to favor a call.

And, as we just learned, market conditions will favor a call if the going dividend rate being offered by newly issued CDx3 Preferred

Stocks is at least .375% lower than the declared dividend rate being paid by your five year old callable CDx3 Preferred Stock[4].

Remember that when a new CDx3 Preferred Stock is issued, the issuing company and the underwriters get together and figure out what dividend rate the new issue is going to have to pay in order to command an initial market price of $25 per share. In other words, the dividend rate of all new CDx3 Preferred Stocks is set such that there is a market at $25.

If the going dividend rate for newly issued CDx3 Preferred Stocks is *lower* than the declared dividend rate of your CDx3 Preferred Stock (at least .375% lower from our prior analysis in order to motivate a call), and new CDx3 Preferred Stocks command a price of $25 per share, you know that the market price of your CDx3 Preferred Stock is therefore going to be *higher* than $25.

Consequently, when looking at the market price behavior of a CDx3 Preferred Stock that The Market believes is going to be called, you will notice that the market price will approach $25 from above rather than from below; that is, the market price will fall, not climb, toward $25 for a callable CDx3 Preferred Stock as the call date approaches.

Rental Horse Heads To The Stable

Let's take a look at an example of the Rule of Call Date Gravity in action.

Hartford Financial Services Group, Inc. (NYSE: HIG) is a $12 billion financial services company founded in 1810 and headquartered in Hartford, Connecticut. Hartford offers a wide variety of

---

4 More rarely, market conditions can also favor a call in the event of a change in law such as the case with the Big Bank TRUPS opportunity explained on page 169.

insurance products and services throughout the United States and internationally[5].

On March 1, 2001, Hartford introduced its Series B CDx3 Preferred Stock with the trading symbol HLI-B paying a dividend rate of 7.625%.

Five years later, HLI-B reached its call date in March 2006. In the spring of 2006, the going dividend rate being offered by new CDx3 Preferred Stocks was about 7%.

HLI-B was costing Hartford Life 7.625%; that's .625% more than the going dividend rate when HLI-B's call date arrived. As we saw in our earlier analysis, CDx3 Preferred Stocks that are costing their issuing companies more than .375% above the going dividend rate are very likely to be called when their call date arrives.

Since HLI-B was costing Hartford .625% more than a new CDx3 Preferred Stock would cost them, Hartford had every reason to call the now five year old HLI-B in the spring of 2006.

And, as you can see by the following chart, the entire world knew it.

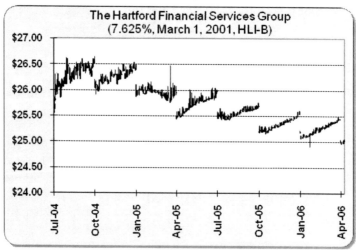

The Hartford Financial Services Group
(7.625%, March 1, 2001, HLI-B)

---

[5] As of December 31, 2010. Source: *www.thehartford.com*

The above chart shows the last seven dividend quarters of HLI-B as its call date approached in the spring of 2006.

You can clearly see the Rule of Call Date Gravity at work here. Market conditions favored a call of HLI-B so its market price trends toward $25 per share as the call date approaches, just as the Rule of Call Date Gravity says it should.

Short-Term Speculators

The market price behavior that you see on the above chart for HLI-B is very typical of CDx3 Preferred Stocks that The Market believes are likely to be called. Earlier in its life, when the call date is still several years in the future, there is no way for investors to gauge whether or not a call is likely. So, for the first several years after IPO the Rule of Call Date Gravity plays no role in the market price behavior of a CDx3 Preferred Stock whatsoever.

But as the call date starts coming into view, newer CDx3 Preferred Stocks that are still three to five years away from their call dates, become more attractive to many longer-term investors. As described in the last chapter, longer-term investors often favor newer issues over those that are close to their call dates since the remaining dividend payout is longer.

The marketplace for CDx3 Preferred Stocks that are closing in on their call dates therefore becomes dominated by short-term buyers and sellers (if conditions favor a call). These are investors who buy at the beginning of a dividend quarter then sell at the end of that dividend quarter hoping to receive a capital gain of more than one quarter's worth of dividend income.

The closer the call date gets, the more sensitive these short-term investors become; buying and selling for, eventually, a mere $0.01 per share gain above what the quarterly dividend amount would be.

Looking at the above chart for HLI-B, you can see the activities of these short-term investors over the last seven quarters of HLI-B's life.

At 7.625%, HLI-B pays a quarterly dividend of $0.48 per share. Notice how the market price of HLI-B rises during each dividend quarter (the Rule of Buyer/Seller Behavior); the closer the call date gets the amount of this rise in market price over the quarter narrows to the dividend amount of $0.48.

Because the whole world knows that the call date is approaching and that HLI-B is likely to be called (which it was), the only investors still buying and selling HLI-B are these short-term speculators who are hoping to make more than $0.48 in a quarter.

This type of speculation is contrary to objective number 3 of the CDx3 Income Engine – minimize work. CDx3 Investors buy at a time when the market tends to favor buyers, sell for a nice capital gain when the market tends to favor sellers and enjoy above average dividend income in the meantime.

During a seller's market (low rates, high prices) CDx3 Investors are always torn between selling their CDx3 Preferred Stocks or holding onto them and continuing to enjoy the great dividend income while waiting for a call.

Are you better off selling now for a nice capital gain or holding on and cashing more dividend checks? That's always the question for CDx3 Investors during a seller's market for CDx3 Preferred Stocks.

Since CDx3 Investors always purchase their CDx3 Preferred Stocks for less than $25 per share, the real question becomes how much capital gain income do you want to pile on top of your great dividend income and when would you like to do so.

Over the last three chapters I have provided you with a couple of tools to help answer that question. You can calculate your CDx3 Preferred Stock's Target Sell Price and just check the market price on the last day of each dividend quarter to see if it is time to consider selling.

Or just hang onto your CDx3 Preferred Stock until the call date arrives and let your "built-in buyer" purchase your shares back from you at $25 per share when market conditions return to a point where it pays them (and you) to do so.

That's all there is to it. Your choice. Until then you can go back to your golf game and know that the quarterly dividend checks from the highest quality preferred stocks available - CDx3 Preferred Stocks - will just keep coming.

Doug K. Le Du

FIFTEEN

RESULTS – HOW YOU WOULD HAVE DONE

In this chapter I will present how you, as a CDx3 Investor, would have done had you purchased every CDx3 Preferred Stock that was issued between January 2001 and December 2010.

> **SPECIAL NOTE:** The data for this book was collected during the spring of 2011. By sending a blank email message to
>
> **Update4@PreferredStockInvesting.com**
>
> you will receive an auto-reply with download instructions for the most recent update to the CDx3 Preferred Stock investing research data presented in this chapter.
>
> To read about other recent tips and the current marketplace for CDx3 Preferred Stocks go to my blog:
>
> **www.PreferredStockInvesting.Blogspot.com**

The investing results presented in this chapter appear in increasing detail starting with an annual summary and concluding with data tables that provide the most complete level of detail for every CDx3 Preferred Stock in the date range covered by this book.

In compiling the tables presented throughout this chapter I apply the buying and selling rules as described throughout Part III and Part IV, respectively, and use the following assumptions:

- Purchase date/price: During seller's market conditions (2001 – May, 2007) I assume that the investor purchased their shares using the Over-The-Counter stock exchange (page 144) for $25.00 per share on the IPO date. During buyer's market conditions (June 2007 – 2008), the closing market price on the first trading day following the end of the second dividend quarter is used as described on page 158.

- The indicated Number of Bonus Quarters is derived using the table on page 202.

- Sell date/price: All indicated Sell Dates are the last day of the preferred stock's dividend quarter. Unless otherwise indicated, a sale is recorded when the market price exceeded the Target Sell Price for each security on that date as discussed in chapter 13.

- Income per share: Includes dividends paid plus the capital gain earned upon sale. Unsold issues are therefore not included in these values.

- Upgrades not included: Issues that would have been upgraded per the discussion in chapter 12 are noted in the detailed tables. But since these opportunistic transactions were exchanges of one CDx3 Preferred Stock for another the results of these sales are not included in any of the totals presented here (average annual sale price, income per share and effective annual return values do not include the noted upgrades).

- Upgrade timing: To reflect actual investor behavior more accurately I assume that the investor would not consider upgrading a newly purchased CDx3 Preferred Stock for at least three months after purchase and only if a dividend gain of at least 0.100% can be realized by doing so.

- Average bank Certificate of Deposit (CD) values are the average of the top ten Annual Percentage Yield (APY) interest rates for a 24-month, $10,000 CD offered by U.S. banks in the month indicated by the IPO Date. Source: *BankRate.com*.

Annual Results

The following table summarizes the number of CDx3 Preferred Stocks issued and sold from January 2001 through December 2010.

IPO Year	# Issued	# Sold	Ave. Days Held	Ave. Div. Rate	Ave. Total Income	Ave. Eff.Ann. Return
2001	35	35	626	7.61%	$ 5.09	12.17%
2002	27	27	408	7.73%	$ 4.10	15.71%
2003	19	18	253	6.96%	$ 2.40	18.31%
2004	13	8	128	6.83%	$ 1.47	15.14%
2005	7	3	295	6.80%	$ 2.25	11.61%
2006	25	13	141	6.94%	$ 1.44	14.83%
2007	15	8	1567*	7.21%	$ 6.92	10.15%
2008	10	10	822	8.37%	$ 9.58	35.52%
2009	2	2	228	8.85%	$ 3.70	24.52%
2010	5	2	157	6.77%	$ 1.83	15.30%

*See the footnote on page 234 regarding how section 171 of the 2010 Wall Street Reform Act was applied to these sales.

Of the 158 CDx3 Preferred Stocks issued between 2001 and 2010 you would have sold 126 (80%) had you been using the CDx3 Income Engine at the time.

Of the remaining 32 issues, 16 would have been upgraded to other CDx3 Preferred Stocks as described on page 187. The 16 CDx3 Preferred Stocks that have yet to be sold (labeled "No Sale Yet" in the detailed performance tables coming up) are issues that were just introduced in 2010 and have not completed enough dividend quarters yet to generate a sale or are issues from the low dividend rate period of 2006 and early-2007 prior to the onset of the Global Credit Crisis.

CDx3 Preferred Stock Performance Versus Bank CDs

The below table repeats the Effective Annual Return column from the above annual results, then calculates how much better the CDx3 Income Engine would have done when compared to the average annual yield being paid by bank CDs at the time.

IPO Year	Average Eff. Annual Return	Average Annual CD Yield[1]	Times Better Than CDs
2001	12.17%	4.72%	2.58x
2002	15.71%	3.28%	4.79x
2003	18.31%	2.28%	8.03x
2004	15.14%	1.52%	9.96x
2005	11.61%	2.35%	4.94x
2006	14.83%	3.64%	4.07x
2007	10.15%	5.21%	1.95x
2008	35.52%	3.62%	9.81x
2009	24.52%	2.28%	10.75x
2010	15.30%	1.86%	8.23x

[1] 24-month, $10,000 CD, APY. Source: *BankRate.com*

www.PreferredStockInvesting.com

Over the ten year period covered by this book, the CDx3 Income Engine would have returned to you, on average, over six times what you would have earned with bank CDs with no more effort than it takes to review your monthly bank statement.

As I've mentioned before, whether or not the lower investment risk from CDs justifies the lower income is a decision that only you can make. But this table shows you exactly what you would have given up.

Detailed Performance Results

The remaining pages of this chapter present the detailed performance results for every CDx3 Preferred Stock issued between January 2001 and December 2010.

In all cases, the investment results presented in these tables reflect the results that you would have realized had you been investing in CDx3 Preferred Stocks since January 2001 using the method described throughout this book.

The CDx3 Preferred Stocks shown on the tables in this chapter are sorted by IPO Date. The effective annual return that you would have realized is presented and compared to the average annual yield rate of a 24-month, $10,000 bank CD available at the time that each CDx3 Preferred Stock became available for public sale (the IPO Date).

Big Bank TRUPS Issued During The 2007 Buyer's Market

For CDx3 Preferred Stocks issued during the buyer's market triggered by the Global Credit Crisis I assume that you would have purchased your shares at the earliest opportunity.

As explained in chapter 10, during a buyer's market the market price of a CDx3 Preferred Stock will tend to fall within the first two dividend quarters. Therefore, for the purposes of these tables I use the closing market price on the first trading day after the completion of the second dividend quarter as your purchase price.

For the remaining Big Bank TRUPS that have yet to sell, I assume that you have the steely nerves of a professional poker player and pass on all future selling opportunities. These securities fall under the provisions of section 171 of the 2010 Wall Street Reform Act and are therefore highly likely to be called by your "built-in buyer." Therefore, for the purposes of these tables, I use the call date of each issues as its sell date and $25.00 per share as the sell price for Big Bank TRUPS from this period that have yet to sell.

You now understand the nature of the marketplace for CDx3 Preferred Stocks (Part I) and the mechanics involved with selecting (Part II), buying (Part III) and selling (Part IV) them.

> **The CDx3 Income Engine**: Use the highest quality preferred stocks to earn above average dividend income while simultaneously creating multiple downstream capital gain opportunities.

The CDx3 Income Engine Summary Table is now complete and presented separately on the following page for your photocopying convenience.

CDx3 Income Engine Summary Table

	CDx3 MARKETPLACE DIRECTION	
	Buyer's Market	**Seller's Market**
HOW TO TELL (Part I)	▪ Dividend rates increasing ▪ Market prices < $25 per share ▪ CDx3 Perfect Market Index >100	▪ Dividend rates decreasing ▪ Market prices > $25 per share ▪ CDx3 Perfect Market Index <100
SELECTING (Part II)	▪ CDx3 Selection Criteria ▪ SEC EDGAR system ▪ Watchlist (one for each quarter) ▪ CDx3 Preferred Stock catalog	▪ CDx3 Selection Criteria ▪ SEC EDGAR system ▪ Watchlist (one for each quarter) ▪ CDx3 Preferred Stock catalog

BUYING (Part III)	▪ New issues > Over-The-Counter
	▪ CDx3 Bargain Table
	   - < $25 per share
	   - Early in dividend quarter
	   - Old issues > 2nd dividend qtr
	▪ Big Bank TRUPS
	▪ CDx3's Beyond Call Date
		▪ New issues > Over-The-Counter
		▪ CDx3 Bargain Table
		   - < $25 per share
		   - Early in dividend quarter
		
		▪ Big Bank TRUPS
		▪ CDx3's Beyond Call Date

SELLING (Part IV)	▪ Enjoy dividend checks; do not sell during a buyer's market ▪ Check for "upgrades"	▪ Market price > Target Sell Price; or ▪ Called by issuing company for $25 ▪ Last day of dividend quarter ▪ Check for "upgrades"

© 2011 Doug K. Le Du. All rights reserved.
CDx3, CDx3 Perfect Market Index, CDx3 Preferred Stock, CDx3 Income Engine, CDx3 Bargain Table, CDx3 Selection Criteria, Preferred Stock List trademarks of Doug K. Le Du.

In the next Part of *Preferred Stock Investing* we will move on to discuss various aspects of building and managing your CDx3 Portfolio to generate even more income and actually become "self-funding." But first, here are the detailed results tables for every CDx3 Preferred Stock issued since January 2001.

CDx3 Preferred Stock Results
Issued During 2001 (Seller's Market)

	Sym	IPO Date	Div Rate	Sell Date	Sell Price	Inc Per Share	Effective Annual Return	24-Mo CD Rate(%)
1	D-A	1/11	8.400%	01/24/03	$ 27.21	$ 5.99	12.22%	5.48%
2	JPT	2/02	7.500%	04/24/03	$ 27.10	$ 5.83	10.48%	5.88%
3	EDE-D	2/23	8.500%	02/25/03	$ 27.17	$ 5.93	12.08%	5.88%
4	HLI-B	3/01	7.625%	07/09/03	$ 27.65	$ 6.70	10.69%	5.78%
5	ATG-	5/15	8.000%	07/29/02	$ 27.00	$ 4.01	13.15%	4.95%
6	GAB-B	6/14	7.200%	03/14/03	$ 27.28	$ 5.04	11.70%	4.95%
7	SPG-F	7/01	8.750%	06/12/03	$ 28.00	$ 6.83	16.14%	4.65%
8	MJH	7/13	7.250%	06/12/03	$ 27.40	$ 5.52	12.94%	4.65%
9	ECT	7/18	8.250%	07/25/03	$ 27.15	$ 5.84	11.90%	4.65%
10	C-V	7/23	7.125%	05/09/03	$ 27.09	$ 4.88	11.36%	4.65%
11	CMA-Z	7/27	7.600%	06/25/03	$ 27.75	$ 5.94	11.93%	4.65%
12	PL-S	8/20	7.500%	02/10/04	$ 27.09	$ 6.29	10.16%	4.07%
13	WSF	8/24	7.000%	11/03/03	$ 26.77	$ 5.31	9.57%	4.07%
14	PSA-R	9/04	8.000%	06/11/03	$ 27.20	$ 5.34	14.89%	3.85%
15	FBF-L	9/17	7.200%	06/10/03	$ 27.53	$ 5.22	12.01%	3.85%
16	C-Z	9/18	6.950%	03/11/03	$ 26.80	$ 3.96	10.74%	3.85%
17	ONE-	9/24	7.200%	04/09/03	$ 26.84	$ 4.20	11.46%	3.85%
18	FZB-	10/05	8.400%	03/11/03	$ 27.50	$ 5.10	13.86%	3.97%
19	STI-	10/15	7.125%	03/11/03	$ 26.83	$ 3.90	11.26%	3.97%
20	DMG-A	10/17	7.800%	04/24/03	$ 27.19	$ 4.71	12.84%	3.97%
21	PSA-S	10/17	7.875%	06/11/03	$ 27.24	$ 5.10	11.80%	3.97%
22	HIG-C	10/22	7.450%	06/25/03	$ 27.03	$ 4.72	10.94%	3.97%
23	USB-C	10/29	7.350%	07/28/03	$ 26.95	$ 4.73	10.99%	3.97%
24	TMK-T	11/02	7.750%	04/25/03	$ 26.95	$ 4.37	11.90%	3.95%
25	VLY-A	11/02	7.750%	05/27/03	$ 27.30	$ 4.95	13.54%	3.95%
26	HI-V	11/02	7.500%	11/11/03	$ 27.05	$ 5.40	10.98%	3.95%
27	LNC-V	11/13	7.650%	06/24/03	$ 27.65	$ 5.29	12.14%	3.95%
28	GUP-C	11/13	7.375%	06/25/03	$ 27.75	$ 5.29	14.43%	3.95%
29	FRT-B	11/20	8.500%	07/10/03	$ 27.26	$ 5.34	12.38%	3.95%
30	WPF	11/30	7.000%	02/11/03	$ 26.78	$ 3.53	11.55%	3.95%
31	USB-D	12/03	7.250%	06/10/03	$ 27.88	$ 5.20	14.07%	3.78%
32	STI-V	12/05	7.050%	03/11/03	$ 26.80	$ 3.61	11.82%	3.78%
33	BAC-W	12/10	7.000%	03/11/03	$ 26.96	$ 3.73	12.20%	3.78%
34	NCF-	12/10	7.700%	06/10/03	$ 27.55	$ 4.98	13.50%	3.78%
35	TMK-S	12/12	7.750%	07/28/03	$ 27.65	$ 5.34	12.27%	3.78%
	Averages:		7.610%		$ 27.24	$ 5.09	12.17%	4.72%

2001 Notes:

1. Historical daily market price data for two 2001 CDx3 Preferred Stocks (BSC-X and STA-A) was not available when this table was prepared.

2. The number of bonus quarters value was 4 for all CDx3 Preferred Stocks issued during 2001.

CDx3 Preferred Stock Results
Issued During 2002 (Seller's Market)

	Sym	IPO Date	Div Rate(%)	Sell Date	Sell Price	Inc Per Share	Effective Annual Return	24-Mo CD Rate(%)
1	DTE-A	1/11	7.800%	04/25/03	$ 27.20	$ 4.25	13.99%	3.30%
2	PSA-T	1/16	7.625%	06/11/03	$ 27.16	$ 4.45	12.06%	3.30%
3	BXS-A	1/23	8.150%	06/24/03	$ 27.57	$ 4.98	13.46%	3.30%
4	BAC-V	1/25	7.000%	04/25/03	$ 26.93	$ 3.70	12.12%	3.30%
5	JPM-J	1/29	7.000%	02/10/04	$ 27.11	$ 5.24	10.63%	3.30%
6	PSA-U	2/14	7.625%	06/11/03	$ 27.17	$ 4.31	11.61%	3.30%
7	BGI-T	2/15	8.000%	06/25/03	$ 28.05	$ 5.30	14.20%	3.30%
8	FBF-M	3/05	7.200%	06/10/03	$ 27.75	$ 4.60	12.25%	3.60%
9	MP-E	3/19	7.200%	06/23/03	$ 26.85	$ 3.71	12.17%	3.60%
10	WPD	3/22	6.950%	06/25/03	$ 27.65	$ 4.50	14.74%	3.60%
11	ONB-B	4/09	8.000%	04/25/03	$ 27.05	$ 3.68	15.26%	3.60%
12	CHZ-A	5/16	8.000%	06/25/03	$ 27.34	$ 4.09	13.28%	3.60%
13	ABW-A	5/28	7.625%	06/10/03	$ 27.38	$ 3.91	16.18%	3.60%
14	BRE-B	6/17	8.080%	06/11/03	$ 27.60	$ 4.19	17.36%	3.60%
15	GPE-W	6/17	7.125%	03/25/03	$ 26.81	$ 2.77	15.39%	3.60%
16	KRB-D	6/24	8.125%	12/26/03	$ 27.30	$ 4.88	13.31%	3.60%
17	EOP-G	7/03	7.750%	02/25/04	$ 27.25	$ 5.07	11.72%	3.23%
18	SO-D	7/26	7.125%	06/24/03	$ 27.96	$ 4.17	17.07%	3.23%
19	ZB-B	8/19	8.000%	05/27/03	$ 27.71	$ 3.78	21.18%	2.95%
20	VEL-A	8/20	7.375%	07/24/03	$ 27.25	$ 3.53	14.48%	2.95%
21	PSA-V	9/05	7.500%	06/13/03	$ 27.00	$ 3.07	16.16%	2.95%
22	HRP-B	9/09	8.750%	10/28/03	$ 27.55	$ 4.59	15.00%	2.95%
23	PL-A	9/23	7.250%	06/24/03	$ 27.27	$ 3.21	17.86%	2.95%
24	KRB-E	11/25	8.100%	11/11/03	$ 27.68	$ 4.15	17.10%	3.05%
25	HPT-B	12/06	8.875%	06/26/03	$ 27.53	$ 3.31	28.95%	3.00%
26	LG-A	12/10	7.700%	11/24/03	$ 27.25	$ 3.64	15.97%	3.00%
27	PEG-U	12/16	8.750%	06/24/03	$ 27.90	$ 3.53	30.73%	3.00%
	Averages:		7.729%		$ 27.38	$ 4.10	15.71%	3.28%

2002 Notes:

1. Historical daily market price data for two 2001 CDx3 Preferred Stocks (CMH- and BAC-X) was not available when this table was prepared.

2. The number of bonus quarters value was 4 for all CDx3 Preferred Stocks issued during 2002.

CDx3 Preferred Stock Results
Issued During 2003 (Seller's Market)

	Sym	IPO Date	Div Rate	Sell Date	Sell Price	Inc Per Share	Effective Annual Return	24-Mo CD Rate(%)
1	RNR-B	2/03	7.300%	11/24/03	$ 26.85	$ 2.90	16.17%	3.00%
2	REG-C	3/31	7.450%	11/24/03	$ 27.00	$ 2.93	16.26%	2.80%
3	WRI-D	4/04	6.750%	03/02/04	$ 26.85	$ 3.03	12.39%	2.60%
4	CFC-A[3]	4/08	6.750%	12/26/03	$ 26.30	$ 2.11	11.62%	2.60%
5	NXL-E	4/08	7.625%	12/29/03	$ 27.10	$ 3.09	17.20%	2.60%
6	KIM-F	5/09	6.650%	12/29/03	$ 26.35	$ 2.07	11.36%	2.40%
7	AMB-L[4]	6/19	6.500%	03/31/04	$ 26.26	$ 2.19	12.16%	2.35%
8	DRE-J	7/28	6.625%	02/10/04	$ 26.35	$ 1.92	16.24%	2.18%
9	HCP-E	8/18	7.250%	03/10/04	$ 26.83	$ 2.50	21.49%	2.18%
10	SWX-B	8/21	7.700%	12/24/03	$ 27.00	$ 2.21	18.47%	2.18%
11	LEH-F	8/22	6.500%	11/11/03	$ 26.62	$ 1.66	29.48%	2.18%
12	LNC-F	9/05	6.750%	12/24/03	$ 26.84	$ 1.96	35.58%	2.05%
13	CRE-E	9/08	7.500%	03/08/04	$ 27.08	$ 2.51	21.28%	2.05%
14	IPL-C	9/10	7.100%	02/24/04	$ 27.99	$ 3.46	29.94%	2.05%
15	PSA-W	9/26	6.500%	03/10/04	$ 25.90	$ 1.33	12.07%	2.05%
16	PLD-F[4]	11/03	6.750%	03/12/04	$ 26.07	$ 1.34	11.05%	2.05%
17	AMB-M[4]	11/10	6.750%	No Sale Yet				2.05%
18	HCP-F	11/28	7.100%	03/10/04	$ 26.50	$ 1.66	29.69%	2.05%
19	PLD-G[4]	12/13	6.750%	12/12/06	$ 25.15	$ 4.37	7.16%	1.95%
	03-Averages:		6.963%		$ 26.61	$ 2.40	18.31%	2.28%

2003 Notes:

1. LEH-F reached its call date prior to Lehman Brothers Holding bankruptcy in 2008 and was, therefore, no longer a CDx3 Preferred Stock when the bankruptcy occurred; all LEH-F dividends were paid by Lehman Brothers.

2. The market price of AMB-M has yet to exceed its Target Sell Price on the last day of a dividend quarter. Further, while the market price of AMB-M has exceeded $25 many times, it has never done so on the day that a new CDx3 Preferred Stock has been introduced. So, for the purposes of this table, it is listed as still awaiting a sale (even though, in reality, it probably would have been sold).

3. Countrywide Financial acquired by Bank of America, no symbol change.

4. AMB and ProLogis merged in April 2011 and will continue business as ProLogis. No symbol changes for AMB or ProLogis CDx3 Preferred Stocks.

CDx3 Preferred Stock Results
Issued During 2004 And 2005 (Seller's Market)

	Sym	IPO Date	Div Rate(%)	Bonus Qtrs	Sell Date	Sell Price	Inc Per Share	Effective Annual Return	24-Mo CD Rate(%)
1	DRE-K[1]	1/16	6.500%	1	11/11/04	$ 25.30	$ 1.31	7.28%	1.95%
2	BRE-C[1]	2/27	6.750%	2	12/07/05	$ 25.03	$ 2.56	7.00%	1.95%
3	HE-U	3/15	6.500%	1	09/24/04	$ 26.33	$ 1.81	15.20%	1.95%
4	DTE-C	5/26	7.500%	3	08/26/04	$ 26.75	$ 1.75	31.96%	1.63%
5	PSA-B	6/18	7.125%	2	09/10/04	$ 26.05	$ 1.05	10.88%	1.40%
6	WRI-E	7/2	6.950%	2	11/30/04	$ 27.10	$ 2.46	20.79%	1.25%
7	REG-D	8/6	7.250%	3	11/26/04	$ 26.35	$ 1.35	8.72%	1.25%
8	VNO-E	8/19	7.000%	2	12/10/04	$ 26.50	$ 1.71	14.13%	1.25%
9	PSA-C	9/9	6.600%	1	03/10/05	$ 25.58	$ 1.09	9.09%	1.25%
10	DRE-L	11/4	6.600%	1	02/09/05	$ 25.50	$ 0.50	10.33%	1.25%
11	VNO-F[1]	11/12	6.750%	2	03/08/06	$ 25.00	$ 1.91	6.37%	1.25%
12	BRE-D	12/3	6.750%	2	No Sale Yet				1.70%
13	VNO-G[1]	12/16	6.625%	1	02/16/07	$ 25.00	$ 2.90	6.79%	1.70%
	04-Averages:		**6.832%**			**$ 26.27**	**$ 1.47**	**15.14%**	**1.52%**
1	PSA-E	4/22	6.750%	2	09/12/05	$ 25.85	$ 1.60	13.55%	2.30%
2	VNO-H[2]	6/14	6.750%	2	11/03/06	$ 25.05	$ 2.16	7.09%	2.30%
3	WRB-A[2,3]	7/21	6.750%	2	02/16/07	$ 25.30	$ 2.41	7.90%	2.30%
4	REG-E[2]	7/29	6.700%	1	02/16/07	$ 25.15	$ 2.24	7.26%	2.30%
5	VNO-I	8/24	6.625%	1	No Sale Yet				2.30%
6	AMB-O[4]	12/7	7.000%	2	01/02/07	$ 25.94	$ 2.44	10.12%	2.45%
7	PSA-G	12/27	7.000%	2	12/12/06	$ 26.26	$ 2.70	11.15%	2.45%
	05-Averages:		**6.759%**			**$ 26.02**	**$ 2.25**	**11.61%**	**2.35%**

2004/2005 Notes:

1. 2004 Upgrades: DRE-K to VNO-F; VNO-F to PSA-I; BRE-C to AMB-O; VNO-G to HPT-C

2. 2005 Upgrades: VNO-H to CFC-B; WRB-A to HPT-C; REG-E to HPT-C

3. BER-A symbol changed to WRB-A on 3/31/2008

4. AMB and ProLogis merged in April 2011 and will continue business as ProLogis. No symbol changes for AMB or ProLogis CDx3 Preferred Stocks.

CDx3 Preferred Stock Results
Issued During 2006 (Seller's Market)

	Sym	IPO Date	Div Rate(%)	Bonus Qtrs	Sell Date	Sell Price	Inc Per Share	Effective Annual Return	24-Mo CD Rate(%)
1	DRE-M[1]	01/06	6.950%	2	08/06/06	$ 25.00	$0.87	7.13%	2.55%
2	FR-J[1]	01/11	7.250%	3	09/28/06	$ 25.32	$1.68	9.22%	2.55%
3	PSA-H[1]	01/17	6.950%	2	08/17/06	$ 25.00	$0.87	7.13%	2.55%
4	MSJ	01/20	6.600%	1	10/12/06	$ 25.60	$1.48	8.15%	2.55%
5	HRP-C	02/03	7.125%	2	10/27/06	$ 26.04	$1.99	11.01%	2.55%
6	USB-I	04/07	6.500%	1	01/08/07	$ 25.58	$1.42	7.78%	2.85%
7	PSA-I	04/27	7.250%	3	12/12/06	$ 26.36	$2.14	18.24%	2.85%
8	COF-B	05/25	7.500%	3	12/11/06	$ 26.73	$2.31	19.63%	2.85%
9	TMK-A	06/05	7.100%	2	12/11/06	$ 26.46	$1.89	15.82%	3.20%
10	KEY-D	06/15	7.000%	2	12/11/06	$ 26.31	$1.75	14.64%	3.20%
11	DRE-N	06/16	7.250%	2	12/12/06	$ 26.65	$2.17	18.31%	3.20%
12	C-O	06/28	6.875%	1	09/26/06	$ 26.05	$1.05	18.16%	3.20%
13	BAC-C	07/27	6.875%	1	10/29/06	$ 26.18	$1.18	20.90%	3.55%
14	PSA-K	08/04	7.250%	3	No Sale Yet				3.91%
15	FR-K	08/17	7.250%	3	No Sale Yet				3.91%
16	AMB-P[1,4]	08/21	6.850%	1	02/16/07	$ 25.28	$1.14	9.38%	3.91%
17	USB-J	08/24	6.600%	1	12/11/06	$ 25.83	$0.83	15.88%	3.91%
18	C-U	09/11	6.500%	1	12/11/06	$ 25.45	$0.45	7.78%	4.30%
19	JPM-S	09/25	6.625%	2	12/22/06	$ 25.95	$0.95	16.51%	4.30%
20	CTZ-A[2]	09/28	7.500%	4	No Sale Yet				4.30%
21	MSZ[1]	10/06	6.600%	2	01/10/07	$ 25.31	$0.72	12.07%	4.78%
22	PSA-L[1]	10/17	6.750%	2	02/16/07	$ 25.28	$1.12	9.27%	4.78%
23	NCC-A[1,5]	10/31	6.625%	2	02/16/07	$ 25.16	$0.57	9.51%	4.78%
24	CFC-B[3]	11/03	7.000%	3	No Sale Yet				5.29%
25	KEY-E	11/17	6.750%	2	No Sale Yet				5.29%
	06-Averages:		6.941%			$ 26.09	$1.44	14.83%	3.64%

2006 Notes:

1. Upgrades: DRE-M to PSA-K;FR-J to CTZ-A; PSA-H to FR-K; AMB-P to HPT-C; MSZ to PSB-P;

2. PSA-L to HPT-C; NCC-A to HPT-C.

3. CTZ-A: See page 68.

4. Countrywide Financial acquired by Bank of America, no symbol change.

5. AMB and ProLogis merged in April 2011 and will continue business as ProLogis. No symbol changes for AMB or ProLogis CDx3 Preferred Stocks.

6. National City Capital acquired by PNC Financial, no symbol change.

CDx3 Preferred Stock Results
Issued During 2007

January – May 2007 (End of Seller's Market)

	Sym	IPO Date	Div Rate(%)	Bonus Qtrs	Sell Date	Sell Price	Inc Per Share	Effective Annual Return	24-Mo CD Rate(%)
1	PSA-M[1]	01/05	6.625%	2	08/24/10	$ 25.66	$5.63	7.63%	5.21%
2	PSB-P	01/10	6.700%	2	No Sale Yet				5.21%
3	HPT-C	02/16	7.000%	3	No Sale Yet				5.28%
4	NCC-B[1,3]	05/22	6.625%	2	10/08/10	$ 25.03	$4.53	6.83%	5.20%
5	UDR-G	05/24	6.750%	2	No Sale Yet				5.20%
	Averages:		6.740%						5.21%

June – December 2007 (Global Credit Crisis-Generated Buyer's Market)

	Sym	IPO Date	Div Rate(%)	Bonus Qtrs	Purch Price	Sell Date	Sell Price	Inc Per Share	Effective Annual Return	24-Mo CD Rate(%)
6	PSA-N	06/28	7.000%	3	$ 19.50	No Sale Yet				5.27%
7	JPM-W[2]	07/27	6.875%	2	$ 25.02	07/27/10	$25.86	$4.28	8.70%	5.43%
8	FTB-A[2]	08/03	7.250%	3	$ 24.32	08/15/12	$25.00	$6.27	7.40%	5.34%
9	C-F[2]	08/13	7.250%	3	$ 23.00	08/15/12	$25.00	$7.95	9.77%	5.34%
10	MER-P[2]	08/17	7.375%	3	$ 22.63	09/15/12	$25.00	$7.26	8.04%	5.34%
11	NCC-C[2,3]	08/28	8.000%	3	$ 20.26	09/07/10	$26.65	$7.05	14.95%	5.34%
12	KIM-G	10/02	7.750%	3	$ 24.14	No Sale Yet				5.09%
13	FTB-B[2]	10/25	7.250%	2	$ 21.32	11/15/12	$25.00	$9.18	11.70%	5.09%
14	WB-D[2,4]	11/14	7.850%	3	$ 24.93	11/24/10	$26.63	$5.56	11.26%	4.98%
15	C-G[2]	11/20	7.875%	3	$ 24.11	12/15/12	$25.00	$7.78	9.39%	4.98%
	Averages		7.448%		$22.92		$25.52	$6.92	10.15%	5.22%
	2007:		7.212%				$25.48	$6.55	9.57%	5.21%

2007 Notes:

1. Upgrades: PSA-M to KIM-H; NCC-B to PSB-R.

2. Special legislation applies to these CDx3 Preferred Stocks that makes them highly likely to be called. These CDx3 Preferred Stocks are "Big Bank Trust Preferred Stocks (TRUPS)" and are subject to the provisions of section 151 of the 2010 Wall Street Reform Act (which is great for CDx3 Investors; see page 169). Therefore, unless the issue would have been sold for its Target Sell Price as described in chapter 13 (JPM-W, NCC-C, WB-D), this table uses the call date and $25.00 per share as the sell date and sell price, respectively.

3. National City Capital acquired by PNC Financial, no symbol change.

4. Wachovia acquired by Wells Fargo, no symbol change.

CDx3 Preferred Stock Results
Issued During 2008 (Global Credit Crisis-Generated Buyer's Market)

	Sym	IPO Date	Div Rate(%)	Bonus Qtrs	Purch Price	Sell Date	Sell Price	Inc Per Share	Effective Annual Return	24-Mo CD Rate(%)
1	MTB-A	01/28	8.500%	3	$14.16	03/09/2010	$27.41	$16.44	72.24%	3.99%
2	PNH	02/08	7.750%	1	$24.25	08/26/2010	$26.69	$5.83	13.86%	3.69%
3	DRE-O	02/14	8.375%	2	$24.90	09/13/2010	$26.24	$5.00	11.72%	3.69%
4	KEY-F	02/22	8.000%	1	$15.74	09/09/2010	$26.00	$13.76	46.62%	3.69%
5	STI-Z	02/27	7.875%	1	$22.87	08/26/2010	$26.20	$6.78	16.97%	3.69%
6	BWF	03/07	7.875%	1	$24.70	03/09/2010	$26.69	$4.45	14.73%	4.46%
7	RF-Z	04/28	8.875%	3	$21.25	03/09/2011	$26.74	$9.93	22.89%	3.67%
8	FTB-C	04/30	8.875%	3	$17.21	08/10/2010	$26.85	$12.97	48.60%	3.67%
9	WCO	08/14	8.625%	2	$19.76	03/09/2010	$28.31	$10.71	56.27%	2.83%
10	BBT-A	09/04	8.950%	3	$20.10	03/09/2010	$27.78	$9.92	51.30%	2.83%
	Averages:		8.370%		$20.49		$26.89	$ 9.58	35.52%	3.62%

CDx3 Preferred Stock Results
Issued During 2009 (Rates Peak, Crisis Ends)

	Sym	IPO Date	Div Rate(%)	Bonus Qtrs	Purch Price	Sell Date	Sell Price	Inc Per Share	Effective Annual Return	24-Mo CD Rate(%)
1	BBT-B	07/21	9.600%	4	$26.00	04/27/2010	$28.69	$4.49	24.22%	2.41%
2	BBT-C	11/02	8.110%	3	$25.00	04/27/2010	$26.89	$2.90	24.83%	2.15%
	Average		8.850%		$25.50		$27.79	$3.70	24.52%	2.28%

2008/2009 Notes:

1. Once the market recovered in 2010 all CDx3 Preferred Stocks issued during 2008 and 2009 were sold on their indicated Sell Dates for market prices that exceeded their respective Target Sell Prices.

CDx3 Preferred Stock Results
Issued During 2010 (Stable Rates, Seller's Market)

	Sym	IPO Date	Div Rate(%)	Bonus Qtrs	Purch Price	Sell Date	Sell Price	Inc Per Share	Effective Annual Return	24-Mo CD Rate(%)
1	JPM-C	03/29	6.700%	2	$25.00	No Sale Yet				2.04%
2	PSA-O	04/07	6.875%	3	$25.00	09/10/2010	$26.40	$2.26	19.06%	2.01%
3	KIM-H	08/24	6.900%	2	$25.00	No Sale Yet				1.84%
4	PSA-P	10/04	6.500%	1	$25.00	03/12/2011	$25.58	$1.39	11.55%	1.71%
5	PSB-R	10/08	6.875%	2	$25.00	No Sale Yet				1.71%
	Averages:		6.770%		$25.00		$25.99	$1.83	15.30%	1.86%

Building Your CDx3 Portfolio

We're very lucky to have you.
- Chuck J.

Prior to finding the CDx3 Notification Service, I was using a preferred stock search program. While the other program is still helpful at times, your program is superior and reasonably priced.
Mark A.

You've learned how to select, buy and sell the highest quality preferred stocks available – CDx3 Preferred Stocks.

And you've seen the types of rewards that are possible from the CDx3 Income Engine – piling a downstream capital gain on top of great dividend income in the meantime.

This last Part of *Preferred Stock Investing* shows you some of the tips for building and managing your personal CDx3 Portfolio. Specifically:

✓ Chapter 16 explains how to use the magic of compounding to get your CDx3 Portfolio to become "self-funding" and shows you how long that is going to take;

✓ Chapter 17 gives you several tips regarding getting up to speed with what is going on right now in the marketplace for CDx3 Preferred Stocks;

✓ Chapter 18 shows you examples of several documents from the CDx3 Notification Service including a CDx3 Preferred Stock Spec Sheet and the CDx3 Seller's Calendar; and

✓ Chapter 19 concludes this book with a step-by-step example of how to use an online trading account to buy your first CDx3 Preferred Stock while it is trading on the Over-The-Counter stock exchange. A real CDx3 Preferred Stock issued by Vornado Realty on April 13, 2011 is used.

SIXTEEN

COMPOUNDING MONTHLY INCOME

So far in this book we have focused on the pieces-and-parts of the CDx3 Income Engine – the criteria for selecting a CDx3 Preferred Stock, how the market price of that single CDx3 Preferred Stock tends to behave during different market conditions and the reasons why.

Now let's talk about how to manage that portfolio as a single machine that continuously pumps out income while renewing itself – a perpetual income generating engine.

In this chapter I will discuss the ongoing management of your CDx3 Portfolio. You'll see how (1) your CDx3 Portfolio generates continuous monthly, not quarterly, income and (2) the miracle of compounding shifts your CDx3 Income Engine into overdrive.

Monthly Income From Your CDx3 Income Engine

CDx3 Preferred Stocks pay you a quarterly dividend, but you'll notice in your portfolio that they do not all pay at the same time; that is, the "quarter" of one CDx3 Preferred Stock will be different from another CDx3 Preferred Stock.

Here is the dividend payment schedule distribution for all CDx3 Preferred Stocks:

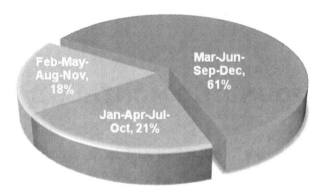

Notice that all CDx3 Preferred Stocks use one of the three following payment schedules:

1) January, April, July, October;

2) February, May, August, November; and

3) March, June, September, December (the calendar quarter).

As you build your CDx3 Portfolio of CDx3 Preferred Stocks, the frequency of dividend income will spread out until you are receiving dividend income each month – not just quarterly.

Also, since you will sell each CDx3 Preferred Stock on the last day of a dividend quarter, and the dividend quarters vary from one CDx3 Preferred Stock to the next, your CDx3 Portfolio will ultimately produce capital gain income each month as well.

Consequently, a mature CDx3 Portfolio produces income each and every month.

The Value Of Your CDx3 Portfolio

As seen in the above chart, 61 percent of the CDx3 Preferred Stocks in your portfolio will use the calendar quarter (March, June, September, December) when paying your dividends.

Because of the Rule of Buyer/Seller Behavior, the CDx3 Preferred Stocks in your CDx3 Portfolio will tend to increase in value as the end of their dividend quarters approach.

Since a little over half of the CDx3 Preferred Stocks in your CDx3 Portfolio will have the same quarterly schedule, the sum total value of your CDx3 Portfolio will tend to increase a little in March, June, September and December. Likewise, it will tend to decrease in April, July, October and January. This fluctuation is normal.

And remember, preferred stocks pay your dividends based on *how many shares you own*, not the current market price. Your dividend income remains the same regardless of market price gyrations. So the value of the individual CDx3 Preferred Stocks in your CDx3 Portfolio is only important on the day you buy them and on the day that you sell them. Until then, the sum total value of your entire CDx3 Portfolio is just interesting math.

Compounding - The CDx3 Income Engine "Overdrive"

Using the methods described throughout this book, when you sell a CDx3 Preferred Stock you get your original principal amount (the purchase price that you originally paid) back plus the capital gain (the amount above your purchase price that you are able to sell for).

Continuously selling your CDx3 Preferred Stocks, re-investing your original principal and pocketing the capital gain as income, will continue to run along indefinitely. But wait, there's more.

We have all experienced the beauty of compound interest – where you buy a CD for say $10,000. An interest payment (say $25 per month) is made into your CD account so the CD balance is no longer $10,000; it's $10,025. The next month you earn interest on $10,025 – in other words, you earn interest not just on your original $10,000, but on the previously paid interest ($25) as well. This is the magic of "compounding."

The same mechanism works within a CDx3 Portfolio. As seen throughout this book, your CDx3 Portfolio generates ongoing income both in the form of regular dividend payments to you and capital gains if you sell. If you use a portion of your gains to buy another CDx3 Preferred Stock you achieve the goal of compounding within your CDx3 Portfolio.

That is, the income being generated by the portfolio itself reaches a point where it becomes enough to buy the next CDx3 Preferred Stock. At that point your CDx3 Portfolio is growing with no additional principal from you. As this mechanism continues this effect starts to happen faster and faster – compounding.

By using all, or a portion of, the income gained from your CDx3 Portfolio to buy additional CDx3 Preferred Stocks, the portfolio generates even higher returns. The CDx3 Income Engine starts feeding itself at an ever increasing pace. You have shifted your CDx3 Income Engine into overdrive.

The Self-Funding CDx3 Portfolio

A meaningful metric is the length of time that it takes your CDx3 Portfolio to become "self-funding" as dividend rates move up and down. The "months to self-funding" metric measures the number of months it will take, given the dividend rates currently being paid by CDx3 Preferred Stocks, to generate $25.00 in dividend income – the amount of money needed to purchase your next share of CDx3 Preferred Stock without any "new" money from you.

So how long will it take, purchasing one CDx3 Preferred Stock per month, before your CDx3 Portfolio begins to generate enough dividend income to generate $25.00?

During periods when dividend rates are relatively low, it takes longer for a CDx3 Portfolio to reach this magic milestone. But the opposite is equally true – the higher that dividend rates go, the sooner your CDx3 Portfolio is going to become "self-funding" where it is generating enough dividend income to fund your next purchase on its own.

Once this milestone is reached, the beauty of compounding kicks in and the whole process starts to speed up.

Here is a chart that shows you how many months, at various average dividend rates, your CDx3 Portfolio will take to reach the point where it is self-funding (assuming one purchase per month, one share per purchase).

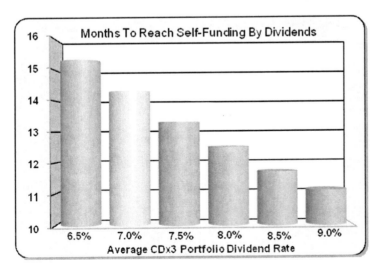

Notice that as the average dividend rate being paid by the CDx3 Preferred Stocks in your CDx3 Portfolio increases, the number of months it takes for your CDx3 Portfolio to reach the self-funding milestone gets shorter.

Historically, for example, the average dividend rate being paid by newly issued CDx3 Preferred Stocks is about 7%. Looking at the above chart, at 7% it takes your CDx3 Portfolio about 14 months to generate the required $25.00 in dividend income for that next purchase.

This is a simple mathematical model that allows us to gauge this self-funding metric as dividend rates move up and down over time.

CDx3 Investors who started building their CDx3 Portfolio just after the Global Credit Crisis already have a CDx3 Portfolio that has reached the self-funding milestone and is now compounding accordingly.

At this point you have learned how to select, buy and sell the highest quality preferred stocks – CDx3 Preferred Stocks – and use them to earn above average dividend income while simultaneously creating multiple downstream capital gain opportunities.

Before you dive in, I have a few suggestions and tips that should save time, hassle and even some money. Specifically, the next three chapters will show you how to:

1) Get up to speed on what is happening right now in the marketplace for CDx3 Preferred Stocks;

2) Start your CDx3 Notification Service (optional); and

3) Make your first CDx3 Preferred Stock purchase.

SEVENTEEN

GETTING UP TO SPEED

I have put together a massive array of resources to help you move forward from this point and well beyond. Appendix A provides a convenient itemization and description of the resources that are available to you as a CDx3 Investor.

The extent to which you avail yourself of these resources is, of course, up to you. The point is to use a combination of resources that will support you and your personal financial goals, resources and risk tolerance in a way that is comfortable for you and your investing style.

At one end of the spectrum you can use the free resources provided in Appendix A and do the research yourself to be a very successful CDx3 Investor. On the other end you can subscribe to the CDx3 Notification Service and receive an email message when there are buying and selling opportunities and let someone else do the research and calculations for you.

What's Going On Right Now

Whether you subscribe to the CDx3 Notification Service or not, you should get up to speed on what is going on with the marketplace for CDx3 Preferred Stocks – the latest trends, issues and indicators - right now.

Always remember that you are looking for the highest quality preferred stocks that you can purchase for less than $25.00 per share. As market conditions (buyer's market or seller's market) fluctuate over time, the list of such candidates will get longer and shorter, respectively, but there are always great candidates available.

Activate Your Subscription To The Free *CDx3 Newsletter*

My preferred stock research is ongoing so I publish two monthly preferred stock newsletters: (1) the *CDx3 Newsletter*, which is free to you as a reader of *Preferred Stock Investing* and (2) *CDx3 Research Notes*, which is just for subscribers to the CDx3 Notification Service.

Subscribers to the CDx3 Notification Service receive both preferred stock newsletters every month.

If you choose not to subscribe to the CDx3 Notification Service right away you should activate your subscription to the free *CDx3 Newsletter*.

Go to www.PreferredStockInvesting.com and click on the sign-up link for the free newsletter or send a blank email message to:

CDx3Newsletter@PreferredStockInvesting.com

and you will be automatically signed up.

When you sign up for the free *CDx3 Newsletter* you will receive an email message that provides you with links to the current issue and to other free CDx3 resources for readers of *Preferred Stock Investing*.

Each monthly issue of the *CDx3 Newsletter* provides readers with last month's CDx3 Investor results, a question and answer article, the CDx3 Company Spotlight where a company that has issued CDx3 Preferred Stocks is featured and special announcements and promotions.

Receive Free Articles From Me During The Month

Like most researchers, I live online. My web log (or "blog") is where I communicate with readers like you. In between monthly newsletters I frequently post articles for preferred stock investors at:

www.PreferredStockInvesting.BlogSpot.com

The articles that I post on my blog are always related to current events that affect the marketplace for the highest quality preferred stock and those investing in them. But don't feel like you have to continually visit my blog site to stay current. There is a great feature on the right side of my blog page that allows you to receive an automatic email whenever I post an article.

Beyond the articles that I post for you, the most popular feature on my blog is labeled "Surveys, Questions – Test Your Knowledge." Each month I post a multiple choice question regarding preferred stocks and investing in them. Click on a question and take your best shot at the answer. You will receive an email message with the correct answer and my comments. It's fun to do and educational.

To help you come up to speed on what is going on right now in the marketplace for CDx3 Preferred Stocks, in addition to activating your free subscription to the *CDx3 Newsletter*, you should sign up to receive my blog articles by email (also free).

Update This Book

The CDx3 Preferred Stock tables in chapter 15 list all of the CDx3 Preferred Stocks issued since January 2001.

As a reader of *Preferred Stock Investing* you are entitled to periodic (at least annually) updates to the tables in chapter 15 as long as this edition of *Preferred Stock Investing* remains in print.

To receive the most recent update, follow the instructions on the first page of this chapter.

The CDx3 Income Engine is a structured, consistently applied method for preferred stock investors. It is low-speed investing more so than quick-hit investing.

Between the free *CDx3 Newsletter*, my blog, the chapter 15 update and the other resources described in Appendix A you will be able to get a sense for what is going on in the marketplace for CDx3 Preferred Stocks right now.

Then decide if the CDx3 Notification Service is right for you or if you want to go it alone. It's up to you.

Watch, listen, ask and learn. Be deliberate. Be patient. Avoid feeling rushed. Start slow and prepare before you invest.

Then invest in the best.

EIGHTEEN

THE CDx3 NOTIFICATION SERVICE

In this chapter I will show you samples of some of the various resources that are provided to subscribers to the CDx3 Notification Service and explain how they are used by CDx3 Investors.

The CDx3 Notification Service is set up to meet the needs of individual investors, brokers and financial planners who have a group of clients interested in preferred stock investing as well as investment groups.

Every major, and many smaller, brokerage firms and investment banks throughout the U.S. are subscribers to the CDx3 Notification Service.

Both individual and group subscriptions are available at what I think you will agree is a very reasonable price. To see current pricing go to:

www.PreferredStockInvesting.com/Subscribe

There are so many benefits and features to the CDx3 Notification Service that I just cannot list them all here. My research into the market price behavior of CDx3 Preferred Stock is ongoing and my data, observations and conclusions are communicated to subscribers continually (but not overwhelmingly) and always in plain English for non-experts.

All investing strategies, at a high level, are the same. You select investment instruments based on specific selection criteria; you buy them when specific conditions present themselves; and you sell them at a specific time when you can expect a significant return on your investment.

As you've seen throughout this book, the CDx3 Income Engine approach shares these characteristics with other investing strategies. The challenge, however, is that most people would rather be spending time with their families, golfing, shopping or whatever, rather than making the daily effort that is needed to select the stocks and monitor buying and selling conditions.

Here are some of the benefits that subscribers receive:

1) ***CDx3 Research Notes* newsletter -** The subscriber's newsletter includes articles about the latest research, trends and tips regarding CDx3 Preferred Stocks and the market that they trade within;

2) **Email Doug -** Subscribers receive a special email address for me. Subscriber messages go to the very top of my email message queue;

3) **The Subscriber's Exclusive Website -** The subscriber's website includes the CDx3 Preferred Stock catalog of CDx3 Preferred Stocks, current market indicators such as the CDx3 Perfect Market Index and the CDx3 Key Rate Chart, and many more resources than I can list here. You can take a tour of the subscriber's website by going to:

www.CDx3Investor.com/Tutorial.htm

4) **Preferred Stock List™ Search Tool** - I personally designed this software tool just for preferred stock investors. PSL allows you to search, sort, slice and dice every U.S.-traded preferred stock or any  subset. Results can be saved to your computer for later analysis, too. PSL runs right in your web browser so there is no software to install on your computer;

5) **CDx3 Discussion Group** – Talk it over with your fellow subscribers. Share ideas, ask questions or read through strategies. This is the largest group of preferred stock investors on the planet; and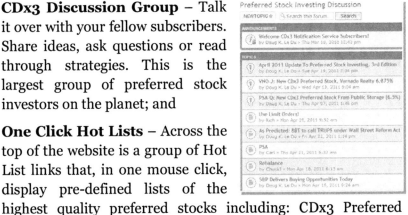

6) **One Click Hot Lists** – Across the top of the website is a group of Hot List links that, in one mouse click, display pre-defined lists of the highest quality preferred stocks including: CDx3 Preferred Stocks, the current CDx3 Bargain Table, Big Bank TRUPS, CDx3's just starting a new dividend quarter and more.

The research and calculations involved with being a CDx3 Investor are done for you. Subscribers to the CDx3 Notification Service receive the results, just the key information that you need, in two types of email messages:

1) Buyer's Notification messages; and

2) Seller's Notification messages.

The remainder of this chapter describes these CDx3 Notification Service email messages that help you make the decision to buy or to sell CDx3 Preferred Stocks according to the CDx3 Income Engine investing strategy described throughout this book.

Buyer's Notification Email Message

CDx3 Buyer's Notification messages make you aware of newly announced CDx3 Preferred Stocks. Every day new preferred stocks are evaluated. Each one is researched and the CDx3 Selection Criteria are applied to find the diamonds for you.

For each of the preferred stocks that meet the CDx3 Selection Criteria you will receive a message when the new issue:

1) Is announced prior to public trading;

2) Begins Over-The-Counter public trading under its temporary trading symbol; and

3) Begins trading under its permanent trading symbol on its destination stock exchange (usually the New York Stock Exchange).

For every new CDx3 Preferred Stock that is issued, a specification sheet, or "Spec Sheet," is produced. A Spec Sheet is a one page document that has the information regarding a CDx3 Preferred Stock that you will need to make a buy/no-buy decision.

When you receive a CDx3 Buyer's Notification email message you will see a link to the CDx3 Preferred Stock's Spec Sheet. Here is the CDx3 Spec Sheet for a CDx3 Preferred Stock from Duke Realty when the new issue first started trading on the Over-The-Counter stock exchange under the temporary trading symbol DREAP.

CDx3 Preferred Stock Spec Sheet Archive History:
Just Announced:02/15/2008
Now Trading:02/20/2008
Destination Exchange, Symbol Change:

Spec Sheet

Duke Realty Corp.

CDx3 Preferred Stock Description

Permanent Symbol	not available
Temporary Over-The-Counter Symbol	**DREAP***
Destination Exchange	NYSE
IPO Date	02/14/2008
CUSIP	264411679
Call Date	02/22/2013

Current Market Price: http://www.pinksheets.com/pink/quote/quote.jsp?symbol=dreap

* Placing an OTC buy order? CDx3 Special Report *Trading Over-The-Counter* – FREE to Subscribers:
http://www.cdx3investor.com/s/vault/documents/specreports/psi_sr.pdf

Dividend Calculation

Dividend Rate	**8.375%**
Annual Dividend (per share)	$2.094
Quarterly Dividend (per share)	$0.523
Payments On	03/31, 06/30, 09/30, 12/31
Beginning On	03/31/2008

Prospectus:

Click on this link to view the prospectus for this CDx3 Preferred Stock:
http://www.sec.gov/Archives/edgar/data/783280/000104746908001448/a2132796z424b5.htm

Need help reading the prospectus? CDx3 Special Report ***Prospectus For The Rest Of Us ($4.95)***:
http://www.preferredstockinvesting.com/xref/xref_pages/sr_pros.htm

Recent Competitor Price Performance (CLICK LINK TO VIEW PRICE PERFORMANCE):

Nov 14, 2007	WB-D	7.850%	http://www.nyse.com/about/listed/icddata.html?ticker=WBPRD
Nov 20, 2007	C-G	7.875%	http://www.nyse.com/about/listed/icddata.html?ticker=CPRG
Jan 28, 2008	MTB-A	8.500%	http://www.nyse.com/about/listed/icddata.html?ticker=MTBPPA
Feb 08, 2008	PNCEP	7.750%	http://www.otcbb.com/asp/quote_module.asp?symbol=PNCEP

Average Div Rate: 8.070% (includes this CDx3 Preferred Stock)

Target Sell Price Calculation: $26.05

$$= \$25.00 + (\$0.523 \times 2)$$

CDx3 Key Rate Chart	:	http://www.cdx3investor.com/s/vault/current/cdx3keyratechart.pdf
Interest Rate Direction	:	INCREASING
Competitive Position	:	STRONG

MTB-A	8.500%	
C-G	7.875%	◄ DREAP
WB-D	7.850%	8.375%
PNCEP	7.750%	

Bonus Quarters*	Decreasing	Stable	Increasing
Best			
Strong			2
Weak			
Worst			

Source: Preferred Stock Investing

© Copyright Doug K. Le Du, All Rights Reserved

As noted earlier, the CDx3 Notification Service does not provide individual investment advice. Whether or not it is best for you to buy a specific CDx3 Preferred Stock is a decision that only you can make once you have considered your personal financial resources, goals and risk tolerance.

However, the CDx3 Buyer's Notification email message will gather, consolidate and present to you the information that you need to make a buy/no-buy decision and in a format that is in plain English and easy to understand.

Seller's Notification Email Message

You use the information provided in the monthly CDx3 Seller's Notification email messages to determine if you should consider selling a CDx3 Preferred Stock.

As described throughout chapter 13, in order to determine whether or not to sell a CDx3 Preferred Stock in a manner that is consistent with the CDx3 Income Engine you need to do one thing: on the last day of the dividend quarter you need to check the market price of your CDx3 Preferred Stock.

If the market price on that day exceeds the Target Sell Price for your CDx3 Preferred Stock, it is a good time to consider selling. That's it.

The CDx3 Seller's Calendar provides you with the information you need, already figured out for you. Each month, as a subscriber to the CDx3 Notification Service, you will receive an email message that includes a link to the CDx3 Seller's Calendar for that month.

Of the CDx3 Preferred Stocks shown on the monthly CDx3 Seller's Calendar, you are only interested in the ones that you own as part of your personal CDx3 Portfolio. You can ignore CDx3 Preferred Stocks listed on the CDx3 Seller's Calendar that you had chosen not to purchase.

Here is the CDx3 Seller's Calendar from January 2011.

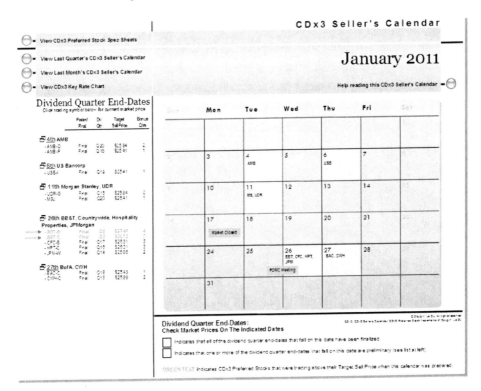

The calendar has the information that a CDx3 Investor needs, each month, to make the decision whether or not to sell a CDx3 Preferred Stock.

The calendar shows you the date to check the market price and provides the Target Sell Price that you are looking for on that date. Clicking on the trading symbol of your CDx3 Preferred Stock will present its current market price. By using the CDx3 Seller's Calendar you are literally just one mouse click away from being able to make a sell/no sell decision.

The CDx3 Notification Service is, by far, the most comprehensive preferred stock information resource available to preferred stock investors. We do the research and calculations for you and you receive a simple email message whenever there is a buying or selling opportunity. Take the tour at:

www.CDx3Investor.com/Tutorial.htm

To subscribe, go to www.PreferredStockInvesting.com/Subscribe

Now let's move on to placing your first buy order for a CDx3 Preferred Stock using an online trading account.

BUYING YOUR FIRST CDx3 PREFERRED STOCK

Whether you are a subscriber to the CDx3 Notification Service or not, the steps involved in buying a CDx3 Preferred Stock are essentially the same. Some of the information that you'll need will come from different sources, but subscribers and non-subscribers follow the same three steps when purchasing their first CDx3 Preferred Stock:

1) Open an online trading account (or use your traditional broker);

2) Identify your first CDx3 Preferred Stock to purchase; and

3) Determine the share price that you are willing to pay and how many shares you want to purchase.

Open An Online Trading Account

If you already have an online trading or other brokerage account for your preferred stock trades that you are happy with, great. Otherwise, I can register new subscribers with TDAmeritrade for a bunch of freebees (usually a bunch of free trades but their offer varies) if you want to open a new online trading account with them[1].

New subscribers receive a special email address to let me know if you would like me to register you for the TDAmeritrade freebees.

I am not affiliated with TDAmeritrade nor am I in the habit of promoting online brokerage firms. But I do believe in giving credit where it is due and the fact is that TDAmeritrade has made a huge commitment to preferred stock trading (their Over-The-Counter preferred stock trading system is the best available).

And opening a new account with TDAmeritrade is free.

While others get the job done, you will not be disappointed with the way TDAmeritrade handles your preferred stock trades and I am happy to be able to get this deal for new subscribers.

When I register you for TDAmeritrade's freebees they will send you an email invitation with the specifics of their offer at the time.

Here's a recent example of the email invitation that TDAmeritrade was sending to those whom I registered. This offer has since expired but this example gives you an idea of what the email invitation from TDAmeritrade looks like.

---

[1] TDAmeritrade's offer varies and is usually limited to new non-IRA accounts opened with a $2,000 minimum deposit.

If you want to take them up on their offer just click the Get Started Now button. You must use this button from their invitation email message in order to get the freebees since this is how they link you to those whom I have registered.

Identify Your First CDx3 Preferred Stock

If you are doing this on your own you can use two tools to help identify your CDx3 purchase candidates. The tables in chapter 15 list the trading symbols for all CDx3 Preferred Stock that have been introduced since January 2001.

Once you have identified the trading symbols for your purchase candidates, look up the current market price for each at NYSE.com. As we have discussed, you want to avoid purchasing CDx3 Preferred Stocks for more than $25 per share.

As shown on page 40, NYSE.com uses the 'PR' trading symbol convention for preferred stocks so PSA-A is PSAPRA at NYSE.com.

For subscriber's the Preferred Stock List™ software tool produced the following list of CDx3's trading for less than $25.00 per share at market close on May 12, 2011. I've rotated the below table in order to make the print as large as the page will allow.

Preferred Stock List™
CDx3's Less Than $25 Per Share, May 12, 2011

IPO Date	Symbol	Preferred Stock Name	Div Rate	Last Price	Yield	Ex-Div Date	Call Date	Moody's	Exchange	Prospectus
11/03/2003	PLD-F	ProLogis Trust, 6 3/4% Series F Cumul Redeem	6.750%	$24.22	6.97%	03/11/2011	11/28/2008	Baa3	NYSE	Prospectus
7/29/2005	REG-E	Regency Centers Corp. 6.70% Dep Shares Series 5 Cumul.	6.70%	$24.29	6.90%	05/27/2011	8/02/2010	Baa3	NYSE	Prospectus
6/19/2003	AMB-L	AMB Property Corp. 8 1/2% Series L Cumul Redeem	6.500%	$24.34	6.68%	06/30/2011	6/23/2008	Baa2	NYSE	Prospectus
12/13/2003	PLD-G	ProLogis Trust, 6 3/4% Series G Cumul Redeem	6.750%	$24.41	6.91%	03/11/2011	12/30/2008	Baa3	NYSE	Prospectus
11/04/2004	DRE-L	Duke Realty Corp. 6.60% Dep Shares Series L Cumul	6.60%	$24.46	6.75%	05/13/2011	11/30/2009	Baa3	NYSE	Prospectus
1/15/2004	DRE-K	Duke Realty Corp. 6.50% Dep Shares Series K Cumul	6.50%	$24.47	6.64%	05/13/2011	2/13/2009	Baa3	NYSE	Prospectus
7/28/2003	DRE-J	Duke Realty Corp. 6.625% Dep Shares Series J Cumul	6.625%	$24.49	6.77%	05/13/2011	8/25/2008	Baa3	NYSE	Prospectus
2/16/2007	HPT-C	Hospitality Properties Trust, 7.00% Series C Cumul.	7.00%	$24.74	7.07%	04/27/2011	2/15/2012	Baa2	NYSE	Prospectus
12/16/2004	VNO-G	Vornado Realty Trust, 6.625% Series G Cumul Redeem	6.625%	$24.77	6.69%	03/11/2011	12/22/2009	Baa3	NYSE	Prospectus
8/24/2005	VNO-I	Vornado Realty Trust, 6.625% Series I Cumul Redeem	6.625%	$24.77	6.69%	03/11/2011	8/31/2010	Baa3	NYSE	Prospectus
4/04/2003	WRI-D	Weingarten Realty Investors, 6.75% Dep Shares Cumul Redeem	6.75%	$24.79	6.81%	06/01/2011	4/30/2008	Baa3	NYSE	Prospectus
10/06/2006	MSZ	Morgan Stanley Capital Trust VII, 6.60% Capital Securities	6.60%	$24.82	6.65%	03/29/2011	10/15/2011	Baa2	NYSE	Prospectus
1/20/2008	MSJ	Morgan Stanley Capital Trust VI, 6.60% Capital Securities	6.60%	$24.84	6.64%	04/13/2011	2/01/2011	Baa2	NYSE	Prospectus
1/24/2007	WRI-F	Weingarten Realty Investors, 6.50% Dep Shares Cumul.	6.50%	$24.90	6.53%	06/01/2011	1/30/2012	Baa3	NYSE	Prospectus
4/08/2003	CFC-A	Countrywide Capital IV, 6.75% Trust	6.75%	$24.93	6.77%	03/29/2011	4/11/2008	Baa3	NYSE	Prospectus
12/03/2004	BRE-D	BRE Properties Inc. 6.75% Series D Cumul Redeem	6.75%	$24.96	6.76%	05/13/2011	12/09/2009	Baa3	NYSE	Prospectus
11/12/2004	VNO-F	Vornado Realty Trust, 6.75% Series F Cumul Redeem	6.75%	$24.98	6.76%	03/11/2011	11/17/2009	Baa3	NYSE	Prospectus
11/10/2003	AMB-M	AMB Property Corp. 6 3/4% Series M Cumul	6.750%	$24.98	6.75%	06/30/2011	11/25/2008	Baa2	NYSE	Prospectus
11/03/2006	CFC-B	Countrywide Capital V, 7.00% Capital Securities	7.00%	$24.98	7.01%	04/27/2011	11/01/2011	Baa3	NYSE	Prospectus
5/09/2003	KIM-F	Kimco Realty Corp. 6.65% Dep Shares Cumul Redeem	6.65%	$24.99	6.65%	06/29/2011	8/05/2008	Baa2	NYSE	Prospectus
8/14/2005	VNO-H	Vornado Realty Trust, 6.75% Series H Cumul Redeem	6.75%	$24.99	6.75%	03/11/2011	8/17/2010	Baa3	NYSE	Prospectus
7/02/2004	WRI-E	Weingarten Realty Investors, 6.95% Dep Shares Cumul.	6.95%	$24.99	6.96%	08/01/2011	7/03/2009	Baa3	NYSE	Prospectus

www.PreferredStockInvesting.com

Determine Share Price And Quantity To Buy

Once you have identified the CDx3 Preferred Stock that you wish to purchase you will need to determine how much you are willing to pay for it (your "bid" price) and how many shares you would like to purchase.

Calculating Your Bid Price

By using your online trading account, or by calling your broker, you can find out three key values that will help you to calculate how much you are willing to pay for a share of your CDx3 Preferred Stock.

The three key values are (1) the current "bid" price, (2) the current "ask" price and (3) the last trade price (the NYSE.com market price values are delayed by about 20 minutes).

The current bid price is the highest price that the buyers of the world have said that they will pay for a share of this CDx3 Preferred Stock.

The current ask price is the lowest price that the sellers of the world have said that they would be willing to accept.

Not surprisingly, the bid value is always lower than the ask value since it would be silly for the buyers of the world to tell the sellers that they, the buyers, would be willing to pay more than the sellers are asking.

The last trade value is usually somewhere between the bid value and the ask value where The Market for your CDx3 Preferred Stock reaches agreement on the current value; this is the point where buyers have met sellers. The last trade value is the current market price of your CDx3 Preferred Stock.

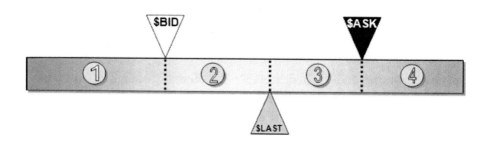

How you position your bid will depend on how badly you want to add this CDx3 Preferred Stock to your CDx3 Portfolio. The above diagram shows four regions. The closer your bid price is to region number 4, the faster it will get processed ("filled") since region 4 represents a bid price that is higher than the ask value.

If, on the other hand, you bid in region number 1, below the current high bidder, do not expect much action anytime soon since there are other buyers in the world who have declared that they are willing to pay more than you are offering in region number 1.

The Number Of Shares To Buy

Have an equal dollar amount invested in each CDx3 Preferred Stock in your CDx3 Portfolio. Doing so makes reviewing your positions much quicker.

If you have $4,000 of this one and $700 of that one and $12,000 of another one, it takes way too much thought to quickly see where you're at compared to a situation where you have, say, $3,000 of each (for example).

Also, for those of you planning on managing your CDx3 Portfolio using an online brokerage account, round your fixed number of shares per purchase to a nice round number like 50 or 200; doing so might save you money.

Unlike full service brokers that charge a percentage, online brokerage services charge you a fixed commission fee (about $10) for each trade. If they can complete your "buy order" in one transaction (i.e. they are able to find a seller to sell your requested number of shares to you), you get charged one commission fee.

If, however, they have to split your order into multiple transactions, you may be charged for multiple transactions (check with your online broker as they vary on this point).

Also, you may be charged additional commission fees if it takes several days to find the number of shares you are attempting to buy. As a rule of thumb, if you are trying to buy more than about 7% of the average daily trading volume of your CDx3 Preferred Stock your buy order may take more than one day to fill.

Generally, you want to make it as easy as possible for your buy order to be processed in a single transaction.

Enter Your Buy Order

If you are using a full service broker for your CDx3 Preferred Stock trades you would just phone your broker with your buy price and number of shares at this point and your broker will enter your buy order for you.

If you are using an online trading account, such as one with TDAmeritrade, you'll be entering your buy order yourself.

Let's say that you've decided to purchase 800 shares of a CDx3 Preferred Stock from Vornado Realty while it was brand new and still trading on the Over-The-Counter stock exchange under its temporary trading symbol VNONP. Here is how entering your order for VNONP would have looked at TDAmeritrade on April 25, 2011.

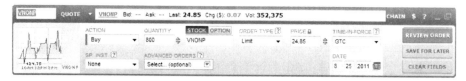

As explained in chapter 9, because of the manual nature of the OTC you will have to phone your broker (TDAmeritrade in this example) to get the current bid and ask values for VNONP (the bid and ask values will be blank in your online system).

When you are purchasing CDx3 Preferred Stocks that are trading on the New York Stock Exchange (rather than the OTC as in this example) the bid and ask values will display automatically; no need to phone your broker.

In this example I have set the quantity of shares to purchase to 800.

Notice the Order type is set to "Limit." This means that you are willing to pay *up to* your bid price (which you have set to $24.85 in this example). A limit order tells your broker's system to consider your Bid price a *maximum* value that you are willing to pay, a limit.

If $24.85 is higher than the current bid value, and very close to the ask value, your order will probably be filled fairly quickly.

Also, when buying Over-The-Counter it may be helpful to set the Expiration field to "GTC" as I show here. GTC means "Good Til Canceled." Otherwise, your buy order will expire at the end of the current trading day. By setting the Expiration field to GTC, your buy order is good for 30 days. This will save you the trouble of having to continually check the status of your order or re-enter it tomorrow if it does not fill today.

After you review your order, you would click the Place Order button on the review screen and your buy order for 800 shares of VNONP at $24.85 per share would be placed.

Since in this example you have set your bid price to the same amount as the Last filled trade there should not be too much trouble finding a seller since this is the current market price for VNONP.

Congratulations! You have just purchased your first CDx3 Preferred Stock and did so using the Over-The-Counter stock exchange.

Other than watching the nice quarterly dividend checks roll into your brokerage cash account, there is nothing more for you to do except check the market price at the end of each dividend quarter to see if it is time to consider selling for a nice capital gain.

You are ready to screen, buy and sell the highest quality preferred stocks, either on your own or by using the CDx3 Notification Service.

You are on your way to building your own CDx3 Portfolio and becoming a very successful CDx3 Investor.

> **The CDx3 Income Engine**: Use the highest quality preferred stocks to earn above average dividend income while simultaneously creating multiple downstream capital gain opportunities.

INDEX

APPENDIX A

RESOURCES

As a CDx3 Investor, there are several resources that you have available to you. Some are specific to the CDx3 Income Engine as described throughout this book; some are free websites, while others are websites that request a fee.

CDx3 Income Engine Resources

I research the marketplace for the highest quality preferred stocks and write to you about my observations.

This book provides you with the foundation – the basic methodology – for screening, buying and selling the highest quality preferred stocks.

In the context of your personal financial goals, resources and risk tolerance, I hope that my research allows you to make decisions that are more informed about your preferred stock investments than they might be otherwise.

While this edition of *Preferred Stock Investing* is the culmination of several years of research, it does not stop here. My research is ongoing and I continually publish my observations in a variety of forums that are available to you.

In addition to this book, I have organized a wide variety of online resources designed to keep preferred stock investors in touch with the key events that are driving the marketplace for CDx3 Preferred Stocks.

Monthly CDx3 Newsletter
CDx3Newsletter@
PreferredStockInvesting.com

Respectable Returns At Acceptable Risk

Purchase of this book entitles you to receive the *CDx3 Newsletter*. To activate your subscription, send a blank (no message needed) email message to the above email address.

The *CDx3 Newsletter* is a monthly email newsletter that provides a wealth of ongoing information for CDx3 Investors.

Each issue keeps you up to date on the specific events that are driving the marketplace for the highest quality preferred stocks.

I provide tips and answer reader questions, make you aware of news events surrounding *Preferred Stock Investing* and the CDx3 Income Engine and highlight companies that issue CDx3 Preferred Stocks.

Activate your free subscription today.

Preferred Stock Investing Website
www.PreferredStockInvesting.com

From the book's website you can access a variety of resources related to preferred stock investing.

There you will find all of the CDx3 Special Reports (see Appendix B) including a 3-page downloadable sample from each report.

You can also access the archives of back issues of the *CDx3 Newsletter*, download free meeting materials for investment groups and read more about the CDx3 Notification Service.

Preferred Stock Investing also makes a great gift. From the book's website you can purchase additional copies from your favorite online retailers.

Preferred Stock Investing Blog
www.PreferredStockInvesting.BlogSpot.com

Investment Group Materials
InvestmentGroupMaterials@
PreferredStockInvesting.com

I use the Preferred Stock Investing blog to post occasional articles related to current events happening within the marketplace for CDx3 Preferred Stocks.

The Preferred Stock Investing blog allows you to interact with other readers, ask questions and comment on thoughts that I and others have posted.

Every month I also post a question to the blog regarding preferred stocks and investing in them. This is the most popular feature of the blog. The multiple choice questions are fun and informative. You will receive an automatic email from me with the answer to the question and my thoughts.

Investment group materials are available for free to members of any investment group or club. The materials are designed to take 15-30 minutes to review in a group setting.

The Preferred Stock Investing presentation materials are available in three formats: color handout, black and white handout (for easier printing) and as a PowerPoint Show (PPS) video slide show.

You can view the *Preferred Stock Investing Slide Show* via an active Internet connection or download it so you can show it without an Internet connection.

Send a blank email message to the above email address for download instructions.

There are numerous preferred stock resources available on the Internet. Some of these sites are free while others request a fee.

Free Sites And Resources

federalreserve.gov/datadownload - You can download interest rate histories for several decades by using this site's download function.

finance.yahoo.com – Check current pricing of stocks, financial news headlines, company information and much more.

marketwatch.com – Provides current market prices, the most recent ex-dividend dates and dividend payment charting.

pinksheets.com – Has both free and fee-requested functionality. Pinksheets provides a resource for over-the-counter trading activity.

sec.gov – Use this site to find prospectuses and a wealth of other interesting information regarding publicly traded companies.

Fee-Requested Sites

The following websites request a fee to access their preferred stock resources.

CDx3Investor.com - The home of the CDx3 Notification Service. You can take a tour of the subscriber's website by clicking on the Tutorial button.

epreferreds.com - Provides information related to fixed-income investments, including preferred stocks.

pinksheets.com – Has both free and fee-requested functionality. Pinksheets provides a resource for over-the-counter trading activity.

quantumonline.com – Provides information on different types of securities, including preferred stocks.

APPENDIX B

CDx3 SPECIAL REPORTS

T he CDx3 Special Report Series consists of several short, single topic research reports that provide additional detail to interested CDx3 Investors.

To see the current issues of the CDx3 Special Report Series, go to:

www.PreferredStockInvesting.com

and click on the Special Reports link. At that website you will be able to view three sample pages of each CDx3 Special Report (page 1 plus two additional pages from within the document).

Trading Over-The-Counter Using The Over-The-Counter Stock Exchange

This CDx3 Special Report is for CDx3 Investors who want to know more about the mechanics of the "Over-The-Counter" stock exchange. CDx3 Preferred Stocks are traded on the New York Stock Exchange like any other stock. But for the first couple of weeks after they are introduced, before the major exchange approves their trading application, they are often temporarily traded in the "over-the-counter" exchange for a discount. This CDx3 Special Report helps CDx3 Investors who are using online trading accounts to take advantage of the discounted pricing that is frequently available.

Prospectus For The Rest Of Us Reviewing The Prospectus Of A CDx3 Preferred Stock

This CDx3 Special Report teaches you how to review the prospectus of a CDx3 Preferred Stock without getting bogged down in the legalese that tends to make people avoid reading these important documents.

Calculating Your Rate Of Return How To Do It And How Not To Do It

This CDx3 Special Report was written with input from accounting professor Dr. Catherine Finger and former corporate finance instructor Mr. Karel Podolsky. It is an in-depth presentation of how to set up Microsoft Excel to correctly calculate your effective annual rate of return on your CDx3 Preferred Stocks. This CDx3 Special Report also presents misused methods to perform this calculation and explains why they are incorrect. If you are serious about knowing your annual rate of return, this CDx3 Special Report is a must.

Dividend Accounting How Dividends Are Calculated And Paid To You

It is important to many CDx3 Investors that the dividends they receive from the issuing companies of CDx3 Preferred Stocks be accounted for correctly. This CDx3 Special Report shows you how to quickly find and interpret the relevant language in the prospectus that specifies how your dividends are going to be calculated. *Dividend Accounting* then presents the formulas used by the issuing companies to calculate your dividends for the partial first quarter of ownership that will result when you buy CDx3 Preferred Stocks.

Who Gets The Money Five Key Dates That Determine Who Is Entitled To Dividends

Whoever owns a CDx3 Preferred Stock on the "ex-dividend date" is entitled to the upcoming dividend payment for that quarter. But how is the ex-dividend date calculated? This CDx3 Special Report explains the five key dates that are used to calculate the ex-dividend date of a CDx3 Preferred Stock.

The method for determining the "Ex-Dividend Window" is also presented. The Ex-Dividend Window is a good thing to know about since those who purchase dividend paying stocks, including CDx3 Preferred Stocks, during this window of time are *not* entitled to the upcoming dividend payment.

Automatic Outlook eMail Sort CDx3 eMail Sorted With MS Outlook Rules

Subscribers to the CDx3 Notification Service receive email messages that let them know when there are buying and selling opportunities for CDx3 Preferred Stocks. For Microsoft Outlook and Outlook Express email users, this CDx3 Special Report teaches you how to use a feature of Outlook called "rules." By using Outlook rules, your CDx3 Notification Service email messages will be automatically sorted into handy folders. You can even be notified with an alert message when a new email from the CDx3 Notification Service arrives.